JESUS CHRIST

For Youth

Updated Edition

06 07 08 09 10 11 12 13 14 15– 10 9 8 7 6 5 4 3 2 1

MANUFACTURED IN THE UNITED STATES OF AMERICA

Author
Robert A. Conn

Editorial Team
Senior Editor: Crystal A. Zinkiewicz
Editors: Scott Gillenwaters, Jason Schultz
Production Editor: Susan Heinemann

Design Team
Design Manager: Keely Moore
Designer: Sheila K. Hewitt
Cover Design: Keely Moore

Meet the Writer

Robert Conn has served the church as youth minister, Christian educator, campus minister, editor and writer of youth and adult materials, and professor of religion and philosophy.

Contents

Session 1
Visitors at the Manger

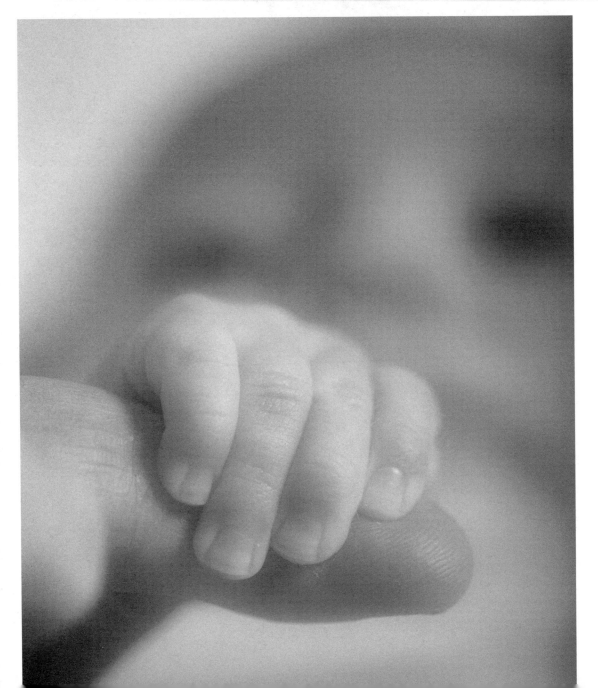

Bible Study: Matthew 2:1-12; Luke 2:1-20

Your church has a heart for reaching people who don't know the good news of Jesus Christ. They are asking everyone in the church to help. You can either write a blog informing your readers of what happened in Bethlehem, or you can write something to go on the church's website describing the events. Include all of the facts, since people who visit your blog or the website may not know the story.

Who? (Who was there? Who saw it? Who did it?)

What? (What truly happened? What did people think?)

When? (When did it happen? Year? Time? Day, or night? Special season?)

Where? (Where did it occur? What was the reason it happened there? Was the place it happened important?)

Why? (What or who caused it to happen? Was there a reason or motive?)

Turn to either Matthew 2:1-12 or Luke 2:1-20. Read the entire story. Then follow the instructions below.

Who? As you read, check off from this list the names of the people who appear in the story in your passage.

___ Mary
___ Innkeeper
___ Angels
___ Wise men
___ Three kings
___ Joseph
___ Herod
___ Jesus
___ Shepherds
___ Harold the Angel

What? Note carefully what happened. Don't include anything that isn't there. Put the events in their correct order.

First

Second

Next

Next

When? According to your Scripture, when did this event take place? During what other significant event?

Where? Where exactly did this event occur? *(City, country, lodging, and surroundings)*

Why? From clues you pick up from the story (not from anything you have learned elsewhere), tell why this event occurred where and when it did. What caused it, for example, to occur in Bethlehem? What was the reason for the event?

It's Good News!

You've done your research; now start writing your TV news report, newspaper article, public service announcement, or blog or website entry. You may not have time to write it out in full, but you can get it started.

JANUARY 6
I Saw Him!

You'll never believe this! I saw the baby Jesus—the one who came to save us! I was in Bethlehem, near his parents' place, and saw three men from foreign lands come. They had followed a star all the way to Bethlehem, hunting for a king.

I watched as Jesus' mother, Mary, showed him off. The men knelt down and offered Jesus gold and other beautiful and sweet-smelling gifts.

When they left, they agreed to go home instead of going back to tell King Herod about the baby. They seemed to think the king had motives other than honoring the Messiah.

I know their lives will never be the same. Neither will mine!

✶ posted by star @ 11:29 (3) comments

The Science News Daily

BRIGHT STAR RUMORED OVER BETHLEHEM

Scientists report a bright star over the small city of Bethlehem; reports from people near the city indicate ...

Gossip Weekly

ANGRY KING SEEKS NEWBORN RIVAL; RUMORS ABOUT DEATH PLOT

Waving his fist angrily in the air, King Herod commanded his troops to find a baby rumored to be born nearby. When asked why he was so upset about a child, the king babbled on about the child taking over his kingdom. The "story" as he told it is that ...

Use the space below for your own report of what happened that night.

Session 2
Visitors to the City

Bible Study: Luke 2:39-52

When Jesus was very young, his parents dedicated him at the Temple in Jerusalem according to their religious customs. Then they took him home to Nazareth. Verse 40 says that the child grew and became strong, that he was filled with wisdom, and that the favor of God was upon him. What do you think that description means? Did Jesus not have a normal boyhood? Did he never get into trouble with his parents?

When they discovered Jesus missing, his parents returned to Jerusalem. It took them three days to find him. What might they have been thinking and feeling while they were searching?

When Jesus' parents found him, he was in the Temple talking with teachers. How do you think his parents felt when they first saw him?

Verses 41-44 say that Jesus' parents were returning home from the annual trek to Jerusalem for Passover, when they discovered he wasn't with them. How would your parents react if you stayed some place without telling them? What can you guess about how people traveled in Jesus' day from the fact that his parents didn't miss him for an entire day?

What did Jesus' parents say to him (verse 48)? What does that detail tell you about their frame of mind? What do you think your parents would have said to you?

Read Jesus' answer to his parents carefully (verse 49). What do you think he meant? Did he not want his parents to find him? Was he planning to remain at the Temple? Was he just being disrespectful? What was he trying to tell his parents about himself?

Jesus went back to Nazareth with his parents. What was his behavior like after this event (verse 51)? Do you think he gave in to his parents no matter what they asked of him?

Luke says (verse 52) that Jesus increased in wisdom and in years, and in divine and human favor. In your opinion, how does this story illustrate that truth?

Hear Ye, Hear Ye

Read the story out loud. Read it first as though you were sympathetic to the parents and thought that Jesus had not behaved properly. Then read it again from Jesus' point of view.

Now imagine that Jesus and his parents were guests on Dr. Phil's TV show (or another television psychologist's show). What questions would Dr. Phil ask of each parent? What did Jesus do that was good? What did he do that was not so good? What skills would Dr. Phil praise his parents for? Where would he find fault with them?

Signs Of Maturity

Here are three checklists. One asks you to identify the signs that show that a person is growing in wisdom; another, to tell what shows that a person has found favor with people. The last is for you to check the signs that a person has found favor with God. Don't spend a lot of time thinking each item over. Your first reactions will do.

SIGNS OF WISDOM

___ knows when to keep quiet
___ can be counted on by almost everybody
___ seems to plan well and have things done on time
___ exercises every day
___ eats plenty of vegetables

___ can tie his or her shoelaces
___ asks questions before jumping to conclusions
___ avoids soft drinks that are not diet
___ is able to learn from experience
___ is careful to whom he or she gives loyalty

SIGNS OF FAVOR WITH PEOPLE

___ is voted president of the class
___ is trusted by almost everybody
___ has a group that always does what he or she says
___ gets a lot of babysitting jobs
___ has a lot of dates
___ dresses like everyone else, only better

___ has a new car that is always full of friends
___ is nearly every teacher's pet
___ gets chosen to represent the school at a meeting in Europe
___ has the best collection of CDs or MP3s in the entire school

SIGNS OF FAVOR WITH GOD

___ prays daily
___ is loved and respected
___ becomes patient and wise
___ finds favor with people
___ never gets pimples or sunburn

___ is able to handle crises calmly
___ gets straight A's in school
___ is able to genuinely care about others
___ seems unbothered by the opinions of others

Session 3
At the River

What's Expected of You?

Parents

Employers

Teachers

You

Friends

Boy or Girl Friend

Brothers and Sisters

Teammates (or Club Members)

Bible Study: Matthew 3:1-12

Everyone expects something from somebody. This truth also applied in Jesus' time. God expected certain things from the Jews, and John the Baptist told them what God expected.

Leaders and common people came to the river to hear John preach. What some of them expected of God turned out to be wrong. John wanted the people to repent (verse 2). What does *repent* mean?

According to verses 5 and 6, who came to John and what did he do for them? Why?

Verses 7-10 tell about some other people who came. They were Pharisees (important people who made and enforced many religious rules) and Sadducees (wealthy priests and others who ruled the country). In addition to repenting (verse 2), John told them to do two things. What do you think each means?

1. "Bear fruit worthy of repentance."

2. "Do not presume to say to yourselves, 'We have Abraham as our ancestor.'"

Notice that John did not tell them to be baptized. What differences do you see in the attitudes of the people who came for baptism and in the attitudes John accused the Pharisees and Sadducees of having?

Which of these two sentences do you think best catches John's meaning?

1. If you want to be God's people, your heart and your actions need to be right with God.

2. If you want to be God's people, follow all of the religious rules and rituals.

Bible Study: Matthew 3:13-17

Jesus came to the river while John was preaching. John had argued with the Pharisees and Sadducees, telling them that they did not truly understand what God wanted. Now John discovers he needs to hear that message himself.

In verse 11, John says that he baptizes people who need to repent. He also says someone else is coming who is mightier than he is. He expects someone to come who will baptize and who will act the way John thinks a truly great person should act. Surely, a truly great man won't need to be baptized himself.

In verse 13, Matthew tells about Jesus appearing. Read why he came. What does he want John to do?

What did John expect to happen?

Thought Questions

Since Jesus was the Son of God, did he need to be baptized?

Why do you think he chose to be baptized? What does Jesus' decision to be baptized say about his relationship with God and how he wanted to live his life?

After he was baptized, Jesus heard God's voice say to him, "This is my son, the Beloved, with whom I am well pleased." Do you think god was pleased simply because Jesus had gone through with being baptized?

Session 4
In the Desert

Bible Study: Matthew 4:1-11

You remember that when Jesus was baptized, he heard the voice of God say, "This is my Son, the Beloved, with whom I am well pleased." After hearing such a declaration, you would expect everything that follows to go smoothly. But that was not the case.

Instead, Jesus had to figure out what being God's beloved son meant. As it turned out, this role wasn't easy. Read on and follow the directions to find out more.

The First Temptation
Matthew 4:1-4

1. Jesus had just been baptized. God had called him "my Son, the Beloved." What happened next?

2. Jesus fasted for forty days and forty nights. What other events in the Bible lasted for forty days and forty nights? What insights do you get from comparing those events?

3. Describe Jesus' condition when he was approached by the devil.

4. When you think about Jesus' condition, was there any good reason not to turn stones to bread? What would have been wrong with eating?

5. How does hunger affect your ability to think, be friendly, or be faithful to your beliefs?

6. What do you think would have happened had Jesus given in to temptation?

7. What does "One does not live by bread alone" mean to you?

The Second Temptation
Matthew 4:5-7

8. In the second temptation, Jesus is taken to the Temple, the most public place in Jerusalem. How is he tempted there?

9. What do you think would happen if a crowd saw Jesus give in to that temptation? What would they have expected of Jesus from then on?

10. What emotions do you think Jesus felt when he was taken from the Temple only to face yet another temptation? What feelings do you have when people constantly put pressure on you to live up to their demands or expectations?

11. How was God tempted at the Temple? What would it have proven had God and Jesus given in to temptation?

The Third Temptation
Matthew 4:8-11

12. Describe the setting and events of the third temptation in your own words.

13. What was offered to Jesus? What, in your opinion, did Satan truly want?

14. Jesus turned down Satan's offer by saying that only God is to be worshiped. Why, do you think, is worshiping God more important than having power?

15. What happens when people seek power but do not worship God?

16. What do you think many people, including leaders of our world, worship most of all?

17. As you consider your life, what things do you worship? (What things seems to be most important to you?)

18. What do you learn about Jesus from this story of the temptations?

Talent List

Below is a list of strengths and talents. Circle the ones you believe to be your strong points. Then put a star by the two that are most important to you. Remember that a talent is not necessarily something at which you excel but simply something you enjoy doing. Feel free to add items to the list.

Being a friend	encouraging others	song writing
playing sports	repairing things	singing
taking care of children	surfing the Internet	debating
listening	playing video games	teaching others
doing math	inventing things	making people laugh
writing	doing research	reading
dancing	being a leader	planning events
being helpful	solving problems	praying
serving others	cooking	
making music	creating excitement	
designing fashion	working out	

Session 5
At the Synagogue

"I Remember When ..."

We all have had to deal with problems. Dig into your memory to recall problems you once had that would fit each of the four sentences below. Current issues are OK. You will have opportunity to talk about some of the things you write here.

1. One time when I needed to hear some good news was ...

2. One time when I felt stuck and needed to find a way out was ...

3. One time when I had a problem and just couldn't see any way out was ...

4. One time when I felt that people were coming down on me pretty hard was ...

Bible Study: Luke 4:14-22

1. At the beginning, Jesus went to Galilee. What is Galilee?

2. While in Galilee, Jesus went to synagogue. What is a synagogue?

3. Jesus went there on the Sabbath. What is the Sabbath?

4. Jesus read out loud from the Book of Isaiah. Who was Isaiah?

5. Jesus read that he was to preach good news to the poor. What, in your opinion, would be good news to people who are poor?

Reread the first sentence you completed under "I Remember When ...." How does it compare to your answer to this question?

6. Jesus read that he was to proclaim release to the captives. What do you think were the captives he was referring to?

   Reread the second sentence you completed under "I Remember When …." How does it compare to your answer to this question?

7. Jesus said he was to bring sight to the blind. Do you think he meant that he was going to cure the eyes of people who cannot see? Why, or why not?

   Reread the third sentence you completed under "I Remember When …." How does it compare to your answer to this question?

8. How do you think Jesus intended to set free those who are oppressed?

   Reread the fourth sentence you completed under "I Remember When …." How does it compare to your answer to this question?

9. When Jesus finished reading, he closed the book and said, "Today this Scripture has been fulfilled in your hearing." Which of these comes statements closest to saying what you think Jesus meant?

   𝑜 Starting immediately, all of the blind can see.

   𝑜 All of those statements have come true, but only the faithful can see how.

   𝑜 Starting at that moment, God was beginning to change the world to make these statements come true through Jesus.

10. When Jesus finished speaking, the people, who were all from his hometown, began to say nice things. But some said, "Is not this Joseph's son?" What do you think they meant?

   𝑜 I wondered who that was, but now I recognize him.

   𝑜 He's from our town, but look at the wonderful understanding he has.

   𝑜 He's just a local boy. Who does he think he is, saying such things?

11. Suppose God asked you to go to your church (or even to this group) and tell them that there was to be freedom, healing, and help for the poor, and that God was going to start the changes all right then, through you. How would you feel?

12. How do you think the people in your church (or group) would respond?

13. How do you think we are supposed to respond to the things Jesus read about?

A Synagogue Worship Service

Today we will worship the way the Jews did in their synagogues. Jesus worshiped this way in his growing years and on the day he stood to teach the people at Nazareth about himself.

1. Sing (or read) a psalm. Look in your hymnal or Bible for "The Lord's My Shepherd, I'll Not Want," Psalm 23.

2. Recite the Shema (Deuteronomy 6:4-5):

"Hear, 0 Israel: The LORD is our God, the LORD alone. You shall love the LORD your God with all your heart, and with all your soul, and with all your might."

3 From the Torah (the Law), read Exodus 20:8-11.

4. From the prophets, read Isaiah 58:6.

5. For the sermon, read Luke 4:16-21.

6 For the blessing, read Numbers 6:24-26 all together.

Session 6
Calling the Disciples

Starting a Movement

You are on the planning committee for a project that you hope is going to be statewide, possibly nationwide. You want to get it kicked off in a big way. Your committee members have given you a list of names of people they think would attract a good following. Which of these would you try to get first? Select at least ten.

Lindsay Lohan	Brad Pitt	Your pastor
Johnny Depp	Oprah Winfrey	Your mom
Garth Brooks	Shaquille O'Neal	David Letterman
P. Diddy	LeBron James	Barack O'Bama
Mickey Mouse	Your governor	A bishop
Your plumber	Your auto mechanic	Hillary Rodham Clinton
The President of the United States	Donald Trump	Aerosmith
Serena Williams	Amy Grant	Your principal
Maria Sharapova	Barry Bonds	Jamie Foxx
	Alex Rodriguez	

Name some others here if you like:

Be ready to give one reason for each of your choices.

Bible Study: Luke 5:1-11

Let's look at this story two ways: First, how Jesus drew others to his movement; second, who Luke thought would be attracted by that story to join the movement (the church).

What Happened at the Lake?

1. What was Jesus doing at first?

2. Jesus got into a boat. Why?

3. After teaching, Jesus told Simon Peter to put the nets in the water. How did Peter respond?

4. If you were Simon Peter, what might you have thought when Jesus ordered you to put in your nets after an unsuccessful night's fishing?

5. Think about when you have been asked to do things that seemed utterly unrealistic. Were they like this situation? How did they turn out?

6. How did the fishing turn out for Peter? Who came to help?

7. If you'd had Peter's sudden good fortune, what would you have felt about Jesus? What was Peter's response? What do you think he was feeling?

8. Simon Peter and his partners, James and John, were astonished. Then Jesus told them something even more astonishing: "From now on you will be catching people." What do you think that means?

9. What was their response?

10. What does to "catch people," or to gather people, mean for us today?

11. In Jesus' time, wealthy and influential people existed, like the celebrities and stars of our time. They included big-name religious leaders, important political figures, wealthy business owners, and entertainers of many kinds. Fishermen, on the other hand, were usually poor, tough, unable to read or write, and had little influence. Why, do you think, did Jesus start his movement by calling this kind of people to follow him?

What Happened With Luke?

Luke was not a fishermen, whom Jesus first called. Luke may have been a physician. He was wealthy and had wealthy friends. Luke was also well educated and one of the best writers in the New Testament.

Luke wrote his Gospel to help others understand Jesus. We know that Luke knew of many more stories about Jesus than Luke was able to tell. He had to choose which ones to include. So, he had to ask himself which stories would help people follow Jesus and join the church.

Jesus' resurrection took place several years before Luke began to write his Gospel. If you were Luke and were surrounded by many well-educated, wealthy people, what would you want them to learn from the story in Luke 5:1-11? These questions will help you:

◊ With which sorts of people are we all most comfortable—those who are more like us, or more unlike us? How would you describe the people in your church? In what ways are they like you or different from you?

◊ Peter may still have been alive when Luke wrote his Gospel. How do you think Luke's friends would react to having a fisherman be the leader of the church?

◊ What might Luke have been telling his friends about true leadership in the church?

◊ What might Luke have been wanting to tell his friends about the purpose of the church and about what they should be doing?

What's Happening With Us?

Jesus called the fishermen to a new job. They were to "cast their nets" not for fish but for people. Persons called by Jesus are to gather other people into the life of faith and the church.

Doesn't that command make sense? When you experience something wonderful, you want others to do so as well, right? If you find hope, help, and happiness in your faith in Christ and in your experience among other Christians, why not tell others? Why not gather them in?

Whom do you know who is not now experiencing a life of faith within a church?

If the person is already a friend of yours, have you talked about faith with him or her? Have you offered an invitation to come to church or youth activities with you? If not, what is holding you back?

If the person is not a friend already, does he or she need a friend? Can you be a friend? Try this:

◊ Greet the person. (He or she may think you don't know he or she exists.)

◊ Start conversations; find out more about your new friend.

◊ Include him or her in things you are doing.

◊ Pray for an appropriate opportunity to talk about faith and to invite this person to come with you to church or to other youth activities.

◊ Follow through: "Cast your net," and gather your new friend in.

Session 7
Model of a Disciple

Who's Lucky?

1. Put a check by those whom you think are lucky.

2. Select the five luckiest.

3. Then put them in order: 1 (the very luckiest) on down to 5.

___ the President

___ new parents

___ the homeless

___ nice people

___ good mechanics

___ attractive guys

___ attractive girls

___ movie stars

___ people who make friends easily

___ people who never seem to be embarrassed

___ the richest family

___ people who can get away with anything

___ the poorest family

___ great musicians

___ "A" students

___ professional athletes

___ successful writers

___ teenagers with "cool" parents

___ high school athletes

___ teenagers with cars

___ people who know how to forgive others

___ people who tell the truth no matter what

___ teenagers with jobs

___ teenagers with happy homes

BEATITUDE
(bee AH ti tood)

means something like

"to have good fortune"
and "to be happy."

Some people talk
about them as
"Beautiful Attitudes."

Who's Happy?

Complete these sentences with the first thoughts that come to your mind:

1. I think people are happy when

2. Three things that would make me happy are

3. I think the happiest people in the world must be those who

4. One thing I did that made someone else happy was

Bible Study: Matthew 5:1-12

Each beatitude Jesus spoke has two parts:

- the name of those who will be blessed
- the promise God makes to them

The blessing they will get is that the promise will come true.

Select one of the beatitudes; then follow these directions:

1. Write the phrase describing the group that will be blessed.

2. Tell what you think that phrase means. (If you need to, check the meaning of the key word or phrase in the "Word List" on the next page.)

3. Name some people or groups in today's world who are like those described in the beatitude.

4. What do you think they are being promised?

Here is a list of those who will be blessed and the blessing they are promised:

- poor in spirit: kingdom of heaven
- those who mourn: comfort
- the meek: inherit the earth
- those who hunger and thirst for righteousness: be filled
- merciful: mercy
- pure in heart: see God
- peacemakers: be called children of God
- those persecuted for righteousness: kingdom of heaven
- those reviled, persecuted, and falsely accused: a great reward in heaven

5. Imagine those people or groups you named in question 3. Where do they live? What do they do? What is life like for them?

6. Describe in your own words what you think their lives would be like if this beatitude came true for them. How would their lives change? What would they say? What would they do?

7. If you were they, what would your feelings have been before and after the beatitude came true?

before:

after:

Word List

Poor in spirit: those who are humble

Kingdom of heaven: the presence of God and the place where things are as God wants them

Those who mourn: those who are deeply unhappy, usually because of a loss

The meek: those who are not greedy and do not demand more of the world than they need

Righteousness: following God's will, especially being fair and doing justice

Pure in heart: dedicated to God; faithful and honest

To see God: to experience God

In heaven: to be with God

Children of God: those who are admitted into fellowship with God

Session 8
The Secret of Worship

Worship Questionnaire

Worship services often include several of the elements below. Rate how meaningful and interesting you find each element.

1 = Boring! (Not interesting or meaningful at all)
2 = Tolerable (Interesting or meaningful once in a while)
3 = Cool (Interesting or meaningful)
4 = Great (Always meaningful and interesting)

1. Music	1	2	3	4
2. Singing	1	2	3	4
3. Confession and words of assurance	1	2	3	4
4. Joys and concerns	1	2	3	4
5. Silent prayer	1	2	3	4
6. The Lord's Prayer	1	2	3	4
7. Announcements	1	2	3	4
8. Children's time	1	2	3	4
9. Scripture readings	1	2	3	4
10. Pastor's prayers	1	2	3	4
11. Offering	1	2	3	4
12. Sermon	1	2	3	4

1. What do you think *worship* means?

2. In worship, how much depends upon what is happening in the service, and how much depends upon what is happening inside you?

3. What would help you be able to worship more fully in the Sunday morning worship service?

Bible Study: Matthew 6:1-18

In the Scriptures, Jesus tells us something about true and false worship. In true worship, we are the actors and we know that God is the audience. In false worship, we are the actors and we act as though people are the audience. When God is the audience, we try to please God. When others are the audience, we try to please them.

Matthew 6:2-4 has to do with giving gifts for the poor. When the hypocrites give their gifts, who is their intended audience?

	__ God	__ Others
Who should be their audience?	__ God	__ Others

What do you think this phrase means: "But when you give alms, do not let your left hand know what your right hand is doing, so that your alms may be done in secret"?

__ During the offering, keep one hand in your pocket.

__ Talk to one hand at a time.

__ Don't make a big deal out of helping someone.

__ Never let anyone know what you give.

Matthew 6:5-6 talks about prayer. Who is the audience for the prayers of the hypocrites?

	__ God	__ Others
Who should the audience be?	__ God	__ Others

What do you think Jesus meant when he said, "But whenever you pray, go into your room and shut the door and pray to your Father who is in secret"?

__ You can pray only in your room.

__ People without their own rooms cannot pray.

__ Don't show off when you pray.

__ Never let anyone see you pray.

Matthew 6:16-18 deals with fasting. Who is the audience for hypocrites when they fast?

	__ God	__ Others
Who should their audience be?	__ God	__ Others

When Jesus said, "But when you fast, put oil on your head and wash your face, so that your fasting may be seen not by others but by your Father who is in secret," what did he mean?

__ Oiling your hair and washing your face pleases God.

__ When you fast, don't tell anyone.

__ When you give up things to please God, don't go around bragging about it.

__ Never let anyone know when you give up something in order to please God.

"And the Churchie Award Goes To..."

MOLLY MICKLER: Molly never misses a worship service, even when she is ill. People marvel at her faithfulness. She is also very generous to the church and is often the first to announce her gift during the annual fund drive. She prays earnestly and quietly for the church. Last year during Lent, she gave up eating lunches and was an inspiration to all.

FRED FREEBONES: Fred has given generously to help many families in the community, although only the pastor knows. (One of the families told him.) One year he gave up his vacation so that he could give the money to the youth mission-trip fund. Fred is also great at praying. People talk about how wonderful his prayers are whenever he helps lead worship. Fred usually practices his prayers before a mirror so that he will get every tone and gesture right. He chooses words that will, as he says, "really wow them."

PERRY PERFECT: Perry has a gentle spirit. He prays often. His heart goes out to the ill, the weak, and those with problems; and he includes them on his prayer list every morning and evening. He also has learned that possessions can become too important. So, each Lent he tries to find out what he has that gets in the way of his loyalty to God, and he gives that up that possession; he does so privately, because the matter is between only God and him. Perry does not give much money to the church or to charity. He does not believe in pledging. But whenever the pastor announces in worship that there is a needy family or that the church needs a new roof, Perry is the first to march up the aisle and put a check in the offering basket.

Word List

Alms: money and food given to poor people

Dismal: gloomy, miserable

Fast: to eat little or nothing

Gentiles: people who are not Jews

Hypocrites: people who pretend to be what they are not

Piety: religious devotion and reverence for God

Synagogue: a Jewish place of worship and learning

Session 9
Finding the Kingdom

Lost and Found

Everyone loses something sometime.

Everyone finds something sometime.

And once in a while, we find something that we have lost. When we do, it's usually something we have missed, looked for, gotten mad about, asked others to help us find, and needed right away. In fact, it seems like those things are what we we lose the most!

Recall something you lost and then found. It may be big or small in size, but it must be something that was important and something that mattered to you. The questions below will help jog your memory. Jot some notes if you need to; then be ready to tell the story of your experience.

◌ Why was the object so important to you?

◌ When and how did you discover that it was lost?

◌ How did you feel when you first knew that it was lost?

◌ What steps did you take to find it? To whom did you talk?

◌ Where did you begin to look?

◌ What went through your mind as you searched?

◌ What worries did you have?

◌ How and by whom was the object found?

◌ How did you feel when it was found?

◌ What if what you lost was a friend or person rather than an object or thing? How would that situation affect your feelings?

Bible Study: Matthew 13:44-46

When telling of the kingdom of heaven, neither Jesus nor Matthew, the Gospel writer, filled in the details. So you get to do so!

Work with either **Matthew 13:44** or **Matthew 13:45-46.** Your job is to take these verses and make a full story that you can tell the rest of the group. Use your imagination. The questions below are just starters.

The Case of the Hidden Treasure
Matthew 13:44

◊ What was the man doing that led up to his finding the treasure? (What was he doing on someone else's land? Was he taking a short cut? Was he a servant or a field hand?)

◊ How did he happen to find the treasure? (Was he digging around? Did he just stumble across it?) And what was the treasure?

◊ How did he feel when he found it?

◊ When he found the treasure, whom did he tell? Whom didn't he tell? Whom was he tempted to tell?

◊ How did he sell all that he had? Did he have a yard sale? an auction? Did he sell it piece by piece? How did he make certain he got enough money?

◊ During the time between finding the treasure and buying the land, he had to get a lot done. This process took some time. What do you suppose kept him going?

◊ Whom did he tell about his treasure after he bought the field? How did he tell them? How did he celebrate, if he did?

The Case of the Purchased Pearl
Matthew 13:45-46

⌀ Where was the merchant searching for pearls? Was he a deep sea diver, or did he buy oysters at the supermarket and open them? Or was he at a gathering of rich and famous people auctioning off their jewelry?

⌀ Did he find the pearl by accident, or had he heard a rumor that a great pearl might be found at this place?

⌀ How could he tell when he had a pearl of great value? What does that ability tell you about this man? Was he experienced at handling wealth, or did he just happen to be a reader of books about oysters?

⌀ How did he feel when he found the one great pearl?

⌀ Whom did he tell about his big find? (No one? A few close friends and business partners?) Whom was he tempted to tell? Whom would he never tell?

⌀ Whom did he tell after he made the purchase? How did he tell them? How did he celebrate, if he did?

Amazing Grace

Amazing grace! How sweet the sound
That saved a wretch like me!
I once was lost, but now am found;
Was blind, but now I see.

Through many dangers, toils, and snares,
I have already come;
'Tis grace hath brought me safe thus far,
And grace will lead me home.

Lyrics by John Newton, 1779

Session 10
The Loving Father

Meet the Cast of Characters

Tax collectors. They were among the most hated of all people in Jewish society. Tax collectors got their positions by bidding for them. The one who paid the most to the ruler got the job. Tax collectors usually became rich by tricking people and keeping part of the taxes they collected. The Jews considered tax collectors unclean and would not allow them even to give to charity, to be witnesses at a trial, or to sit and eat with other Jews.

Sinners. People were judged sinners if they did not obey the Law (Torah) and the many other religious rules followed by all faithful Jews. Sinners had to go through special religious services in order to be forgiven and cleansed. Otherwise, good Jews could not associate with them.

Pharisees. These men were devoted to living their religion as faithfully as possible. The Pharisees carefully followed the Law and the rules of the Jewish religion, gave generously of their possessions, and tried to remain pure. They were laymen who often had small businesses. The common people respected them highly.

Scribes. Honored and well educated teachers of the Jewish law, scribes gave advice about the law. Students underwent a long education and had to demonstrate a lot of knowledge before they could be accepted as scribes. The common people respected the scribes so highly that they often stood in the streets as scribes passed by. Scribes had seats of honor in the synagogues.

The father. The father was a wealthy landowner and farmer. He had many servants. He followed the law and willingly divided his land between his sons as the law said.

The younger son. He grew restless with farm life and wanted out. Jewish law gave him the right to have one-third of his father's possessions as an inheritance.

The older son. Jewish law gave the oldest son two-thirds of his father's wealth. Along with that inheritance came the responsibility of caring for the remaining family.

Bible Study: Luke 15:1-2, 11-32

View From the Outer Circle

You are scribes and Pharisees. Now imagine yourselves on the day Jesus told the story of the loving father.

Even though you know that Jesus has gotten quite close to the tax collectors and sinners, you've heard about his reputation as a good teacher. You respect wisdom, and you're curious. As Jesus tells the story, you begin to suspect that something is wrong. At least, something doesn't fit with the way you have been taught.

✿ Who, in the story, does Jesus seem to say the tax collectors and sinners are like?

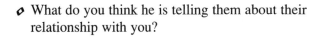

ø According to your beliefs as scribes and Pharisees, what should happen to the younger son?

ø As Jesus finishes the story, you become more aware of the sinners and tax collectors in the inner circle around Jesus. What do you think Jesus is telling you about your relationship with them?

ø According to your beliefs as scribes and Pharisees, what should the father do when the boy returns home?

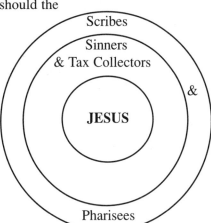

ø What do you think he is telling them about their relationship with you?

ø If the father is a symbol for God, how do you think God treats tax collectors and sinners?

ø What Jesus is telling you both about God's relationship with you?

ø What is your opinion of Jesus when you hear him telling everyone that the father (God) accepted his son (tax collectors and sinners) back with joy, even before the son had a chance to ask forgiveness for his sin?

ø When Jesus tells the second part of his story, you discover that Jesus thinks you are like the older son. Do you think the father treated the older son fairly, or unfairly? Why?

ø If the older son stands for you, do you think you are being treated fairly?

View From the Inner Circle

As a tax collector, you have not been a religious person all your life. But you were brought up by religious parents, and you have often felt a little guilty about not observing the religious laws.

On the other hand, being a tax collector has paid off pretty well. People don't like you; but, hey, you can buy nearly everything you want.

You have found a strange thing today, however. A rabbi (Jewish teacher) has started talking to you. (This situation is strange, because no religious person is supposed to have anything to do with you). He has begun telling a story.

At first it seems like another story in which there are bad guys and good guys—and you can easily tell that the bad guy in the story (the younger son) is supposed to represent you.

⟡ Knowing that religious people don't like you and that the younger son in the story stands for you, what do you expect to happen to the younger son?

⟡ The younger son ends up feeding pigs (which are considered unclean by the Jews). Why, do you think, does Jesus use "feeding pigs" to describe your situation?

⟡ When Jesus starts to tell about the younger son going home, what do you expect to have happen when he gets there?

⟡ When the younger son arrives home, how does he feel about the way his father greets him?

⟡ If the younger son represents you, does this story indicate the way you think God will greet you? Why, or why not?

⟡ When Jesus starts to tell about the older son, you become aware of the scribes and Pharisees standing around you. What do you think Jesus is telling you about your relationship with them?

⟡ What is he telling them about their relationship with you?

⟡ What is he telling you both about God's relationship with you?

Session 11
The Good Samaritan

Meet the Cast of Characters

The lawyer. This man was not like a present-day lawyer, who specializes in the laws of the land. He specialized in the Law of Moses. He was probably also a Pharisee, for the Pharisees took the Law seriously. They studied it and preserved many of the important teachings about it. When a lawyer like this asked, "Who is my neighbor?" he wanted to know if the person who answered his question truly knew the Law and the teachings of the Jews.

The priest. The priests served in the Temple in Jerusalem. According to Jewish law, a priest who touched a dead person made himself unclean. He could not serve as a priest until he had gone through a long period of cleansing. Therefore, if there was any doubt about whether a person were alive or dead, the priests dared not risk touching the body. This priest may have been on his way to take his turn serving at the Temple, and he could not have served if he were unclean.

The Levite. He was a member of the tribe of Levi, who also served in the Temple. Levites were not priests, but they could do some of the lesser services and duties. Their income often came from the tithes (offerings) that they were given for their work in the Temple. Like the priests, they could not serve in the Temple if they were unclean. So the Levite too dared not risk touching a person who might be dead.

The Samaritan. Originally Jews, the people who lived in Samaria continued to use the first five books of the Bible (Torah) as the basis of their religion. Foreigners settled in their land and, after a while, began to marry and have families with the Samaritans. From that time on, Jews regarded them as impure. Great hatred existed between Jews and Samaritans. Samaritans refused to worship at the Temple in Jerusalem and would not even give water to a Jewish pilgrim walking through Samaria on the way to the Temple. The Jews, for their part, were equally harsh and used the word *Samaritan* as a swear word.

Bible Study: Luke 10:25-26

Meet the Lawyer
Luke 10:25-26
Be the young lawyer who has approached Jesus. What made you decide to go to Jesus to ask your question?

___ Just curiosity

___ A sincere desire to know what the Law teaches about "Who is my neighbor?"

___ A plan to trick Jesus and show that he doesn't truly know the Law

___ To enjoy careful argument with a good opponent, like any good lawyer would

Why did you call Jesus "Teacher"?

___ It was flattery, to get him off guard.

___ Jesus is called "rabbi," which means "teacher."

___ I knew he did not have as good an education as I had, and calling him "Teacher" was a putdown.

___ I wished to show respect for his wisdom; after all, he had a wonderful reputation for wisdom and clear thinking.

The answer Jesus gave you was one that you had heard all of your life. He told you to love God and to love your neighbor. But you went on to ask him, "Who is my neighbor?" Why did you do so?

___ His answer was so common that anyone could have said it. I wanted to find out if Jesus had any original thoughts.

___ In any area with so many kinds of people, it isn't always easy to tell who your neighbor is and who your enemy is; I wanted to learn how to tell.

___ We have many enemies who never treat us kindly. I truly need to know how I can tell whom to trust as my neighbor.

___ There is clear teaching in our law. Only Jews are our neighbors. I wanted to see if he knew that rule.

Walk in Their Shoes
Luke 10:30-35

There is an old saying: You don't understand other people until you've walked in their shoes for a while. What would it be like to be one of the characters in Jesus' story of the good Samaritan? Imagining one of those experiences could help you understand the parable and help make clear the story's message to us.

1. **Be the wounded man.** Retell the story in first person. These questions will help you: Where were you going? What happened to you? What did you think after you were hurt? What went through your mind as you saw a priest from your own Temple coming down the road? What did you think when he passed you by? How about the Levite? What did you expect when you looked again and saw a Samaritan coming? What did you think when he came to your aid? Did you want him to touch you? How did your mind change about Samaritans?

2. **Be the priest.** Retell the story in first person. These questions will help you: Where were you going? What had you been doing? When did you first notice the man lying by the side of the road? What went through your mind when you saw him there? Did you think of the commandment to love your neighbor? What prevented you from helping your fellow Jew at this time? How did you feel, having to pass by the side of the road and leave him there?

3. **Be the Levite.** Retell the story in first person. These questions will help you: What do you do for a living? Where were you when you saw him? You know that you should love your neighbor; what prevented you from helping this man?

4. Be the Samaritan. Retell the story in first person. These questions will help you: When you are on the road to Jericho and you see a wounded man, what is your first thought? When you look closer you see that he is a Jew; what do you think then? You can't tell whether he is alive or dead; why do you reach out to him? How do you feel, knowing that you have touched a person who is unclean to you (a Jew) and that you are now unclean as well? In your mind you know two commandments of the Law—one to love your neighbor and another to remain pure. You had to choose between the two. Why did you choose the one you did?

Back to the Lawyer
Luke 10:36-37

You have asked Jesus your question, and he has told you the story of the good Samaritan as his answer. Jesus asks you a question now: Which of these three proved a neighbor to the man who fell among robbers? What is your answer?

How do you feel when Jesus uses a Samaritan to show you how to follow the law and be a neighbor?

___ Just wonderful. I always wanted to know who my neighbor is, and now I know.

___ Terrible. How dare he hold up a lousy Samaritan as an example to me?

___ Excited. I have a brand new insight into what neighborliness means.

___ Frightened. I don't think I have what it takes to be that kind of neighbor.

Jesus then tells you to go and do likewise. Do you do so? Why, or why not?

Session 12
Nicodemus

Bible Study: John 3:1-15

Jesus is talking with Nicodemus, a leader of the Jews. What does Nicodemus ask Jesus? What does Jesus ask Nicodemus? Write the questions and the answers below. Some of the questions are not answered directly in the Scripture. What do you think would be the answers given?

JESUS

Questions   Answers

NICODEMUS

Questions   Answers

What do you think these two sayings of Jesus mean?

1. "What is born of the flesh is flesh, and what is born of the Spirit is spirit" (verse 6).

Verses 14-15 refer to an episode in the Old Testament (**Numbers 21:4-9**). The Israelites had sinned greatly and were punished by deadly snake bites. When the people cried out, sorry for their sin, God told Moses to make a serpent out of bronze and lift it high on a pole. Whenever a snake bit someone, that person would look in faith at the bronze serpent and live. God had provided a means of forgiveness and healing. It required only the faith of people.

2. "The wind blows where it chooses, and you hear the sound of it, but you do not know where it comes from or where it goes. So it is with everyone who is born of the Spirit" (verse 8).

3. What do you think Jesus means in verses 14-15 when he says, "And just as Moses lifted up the serpent in the wilderness, so must the Son of Man be lifted up, that whoever believes in him may have eternal life"?

What Do You Think He Meant?

Read the verses listed below from John Chapter 3. Write a letter N if you agree that the answer explains the verse correctly, and a letter D if you disagree with the answer. You may find yourself agreeing with more than one sentence.

In verse 2, Nicodemus visits Jesus at night because

__ he just got off from work;

__ he didn't want anyone to see him;

__ John used darkness to symbolize Nicodemus's ignorance;

__ it probably means nothing at all.

Read what Nicodemus says to Jesus in verse 2. When he addresses Jesus in this way, Nicodemus is trying to

__ get into Jesus' confidence;

__ prepare a trap;

__ let Jesus know that he has been watching him for a while;

__ show respect for Jesus, whom he regards as a teacher like himself.

Read verse 3. Jesus tells Nicodemus that he must be born from above. The phrase "from above" could also be translated as

__ "again."

__ "anew."

__ "afresh."

__ "miraculously."

In verse 5 when Jesus speaks of being born of water and the Spirit, he means

__ you have to be baptized;

__ you don't have to be baptized, the Spirit will take care of everything;

__ baptism by water is important, but God's Spirit must also be in your life;

__ the kingdom of God is only for spirits.

Read verses 9-10. You can tell from the way Jesus answers Nicodemus that he intends to

__ insult him.

__ tease him.

__ inform him.

__ keep a good conversation going.

In verse 11 Jesus uses the word *we*. To whom is he referring?

__ Nicodemus and himself

__ all truly religious people

__ the disciples and Jesus

Read verse 12. Jesus refers to "earthly" and "heavenly things." By those words he means

__ water and Spirit;

__ things that are easy to believe and things that are more difficult to believe;

__ truths about earthly life and about the kingdom of God;

__ himself and Nicodemus.

In verse 13, Jesus means

___ that he is the Son of Man;

___ that he started out in heaven and will end up there;

___ no one but Jesus will go to heaven;

___ no one is better able to help others experience heaven.

The meaning of this entire passage can be summed up this way:

___ Nicodemus and Jesus had a good debate, but nothing was settled.

___ Intelligent Jews appreciated Jesus, but they didn't always understand him.

___ Jesus respected the wise teachers of the Jewish faith, but knew that his ideas went beyond theirs.

___ Jesus brought the chance for a fresh beginning to people, and it would come to people if they believed in him, even if they didn't understand it.

Extreme Makeover

You've seen those commercials that show before-and-after shots. Someone's going bald; then the same person has a full head of hair. Someone looks pitiful then, after the great makeover, is completely different (and, of course, smiling).

You probably don't need more hair or a makeover. But aren't there some "befores and afters" you would like in your life? What would you like to change about yourself? Remember that when Jesus said, "You must be born again," he was telling us all that we can start over, start fresh, and start out anew with help from above.

In the box labeled "Before," draw a symbol of some part of your life you'd like to get behind you, such as a habit, an embarrassing experience that keeps cropping up, an argument with a friend, or something you perceive as a failing. (For example, you might draw an alarm clock jangling to show a habit of being late, or a school paper with a bad grade).

In the box entitled "After," draw a symbol of what you might do or how you would feel if you could get a fresh start and do it right this time. You might show the alarm clock set earlier or the paper with a gold star on it.

BEFORE	AFTER

Session 13

Men and Women

In Jesus' Time

Put a check by the statements below that you think are true.

In Jesus' time:

1. __ Women in religious families of Jerusalem stayed in the house almost all of the time.

2. __ In Jerusalem, a groom didn't see his bride with her head uncovered until the day of their wedding.

3. __ The royal families were the least religious, and royal women had the greatest freedom.

4. __ Even young women from religious families could go to two dances each year.

5. __ Sometimes husbands and wives could work together at a trade.

6. __ Husbands and wives could work together in the fields, but wives could not talk with passers-by.

7. __ The wealth of the father passed only to the sons.

8. __ Women often married before they were twelve years old.

9. __ Girls under twelve and a half had to marry whomever their fathers chose for them.

10. __ Cousins were able to marry each other.

11. __ Girls over twelve and a half could not be forced to marry.

12. __ In Jerusalem, fathers could sell their daughters under twelve into slavery.

13. __ Men often had to pay a woman's father for the right to marry her.

14. __ Men and women, once engaged, were treated like husband and wife.

15. __ In general, women were viewed as the property of men.

16. __ A married couple lived with the groom's family.

17. __ A husband owned whatever his wife earned or received as a gift.

18. __ A husband could force his wife to make a vow.

19. __ If a husband forced his wife to make a vow that violated her reputation or that of her family, she could divorce him.

20. __ In case of danger to the family, the husband had to be saved first.

21. __ If a husband was not satisfied with his wife and also did not want a divorce, he could take a second wife into his home.

22. __ Marriage contracts included clauses telling how much the husband had to give the wife if he divorced her.

23. __ When marriages broke up, the children usually went with their father.

24. __ When a woman became a widow, she had to either marry her husband's brother or else get permission from the brother to marry someone else.

25. __ Women generally did not study the Torah (the first five books of the Bible, which the Jews regarded as the most holy of books).

26. __ Schools were only for boys.

27. __ Women were permitted to enter the synagogue.

28. __ Some girls were allowed to study Greek.

29. __ For forty days after they gave birth to a boy and eighty days after they gave birth to a girl, women could not enter the Temple in Jerusalem.

30. __ Only men could teach in the synagogues.

31. __ When a Jewish woman left her home in Jerusalem, she was expected to wear two veils, a head band, and a hair net to keep her features completely hidden.

32. __ Rabbis were not expected to have women as students or women in their groups.

33. __ In their homes unmarried women were confined to the innermost areas; their mothers could go into the outer rooms.

34. __ In general, rural people were not so strict about the roles of men and women as city people were.

35. __ Generally, unmarried men were not alone with women outside the men's families.

Bible Study

Read the three Bible stories below. As you do, keep track of anything in them that breaks the rules for men and women listed in "In Jesus' Time."

Luke 10:38-42

✎ If you were a follower of Jesus back then, what might you have learned from witnessing this exchange?

Mark 7:24-30

✎ If you were a follower of Jesus back then, what might you have learned from witnessing this exchange?

Mark 14:3-9

◊ If you were a follower of Jesus then, what might you have learned from seeing this event?

In these stories, Jesus has treated the relationship between women and men in a new way. In your own words, tell what that new way is. How would it improve life for both men and women?

What do these stories say to you, a follower of Jesus today?

If our society were to follow Jesus, what changes would there be in how women today would be treated?

Something Extra

Check out John 4:1-42. Jesus was constantly turning social rules upside down. Even the disciples who were closest to him were surprised (verse 27).

Session 14
The Wealthy

Lifestyles of the Famous and Wealthy

Most of us aren't wealthy, although some of us are. But all of us have some idea about rich people. Think of those sleek, slim, and well-to-do people on TV shows, in the movies, or in magazines. Think about fast cars, jet planes, servants, polo ponies, plasma-screen TVs, and all the high-tech gadgets anyone could want.

Think about yourself with all that glitter and glitz. Let your mind go, and complete these sentences:

🖉 When I think about having all of that money, it makes me feel

🖉 The first five things I'd buy are

🖉 If I had all of that money, my clothes would be

🖉 When it comes to transportation, you'd never see me in anything less than a

🖉 I think I would hire someone to

🖉 For a person with a lot of money, I think the most important thing is

🖉 Of course, if I became rich, some of my friends would

🖉 One thing I would worry about if I were rich is

🖉 Something I have always wondered about those rich people in movies and on television is

🖉 Sometimes, when I see the lifestyles of rock stars and others, it makes me think

🖉 Still, all things considered, it is better by far to be wealthy than not to be wealthy. (yes/no)

Rich Roleplays

- The rich young man had a lot of wealth. His problem was that he worshiped his money more than he was willing to worship Jesus. Think of a modern-day parallel that describes this condition, and act out this scenario.

- Zacchaeus had been a regular tax collector, cheating people out of a lot of money. He was, after meeting Jesus, willing to give back to those whom he had cheated and live a life in light of Jesus' teachings. Think of a modern-day parallel that describes this condition, and act out this scenario.

Bible Study: Luke 19:1-10

Jesus and the Wealthy Tax Collector

Check all of the following statements that are true about Zacchaeus:

__ He was rich.

__ He was an upright business man.

__ He was excited to see Jesus.

__ He could stand on his tip-toes and see Jesus over the heads of the crowd.

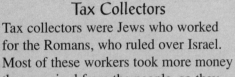

Tax Collectors

Tax collectors were Jews who worked for the Romans, who ruled over Israel. Most of these workers took more money than required from the people, so they became rich while the people became poorer. The people hated them.

Zacchaeus planned on seeing Jesus. Do you think he expected Jesus to see him? Why, or why not?

If you had been Zacchaeus, what would have been your first reaction when Jesus saw you and told you to come down?

Some people who saw what happened grumbled. Why did they complain?

In the presence of Jesus, Zacchaeus pledged to make a change in his life and business dealings. What did he say he would do?

Jesus said, "Today salvation has come to this house." Which of these comes closest to what you think Jesus meant?

___ I, Jesus, have come to visit your home.

___ God's grace is there for you; you show you have accepted it in your willingness to change and make up for your cheating in the past.

___ You have learned to possess wealth without being possessed by it; you have shown that you understand what God wants.

Jesus indicated that Zacchaeus has been among the "lost." What do you think Jesus meant?

Jesus and the Rich Young Man
Mark 10:17-25

Here's another story where Jesus deals out some surprises.

⌀ From what you read in verse 17, what would you say was the young man's attitude toward Jesus? What evidence do you have?

⌀ Do you think the young man's question was sincere (yes/no)? Why?

⌀ Read the answer Jesus gave the young man in verse 19. Do you think that following the commandments is what God requires of all who wish to have eternal life?

⌀ The young man said that he had kept the commandments. How then did Jesus feel about him?

⌀ Read all of verses 21-22. What did Jesus tell the young man?

⌀ Why, do you think, did Jesus tell him what he did?

⌀ Why did the young man go away unhappy?

⌀ Read verses 23-25. What do you think Jesus is saying about wealth?

⌀ Why, do you think, would this statement have surprised the disciples?

Thought Question

Jesus met two wealthy men. One he told to sell what he had, give it to the poor, and come and follow him. The other he allowed to keep his wealth (although the man chose to give half his wealth to the poor), did not ask him to become a disciple, and announced that salvation had come to him. What, in your opinion, is the reason these two rich men were treated differently?

Session 15
The Ill

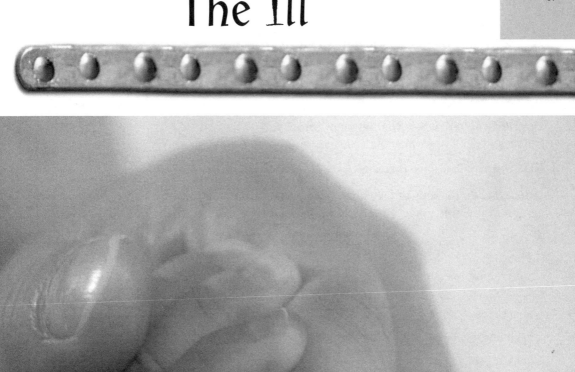

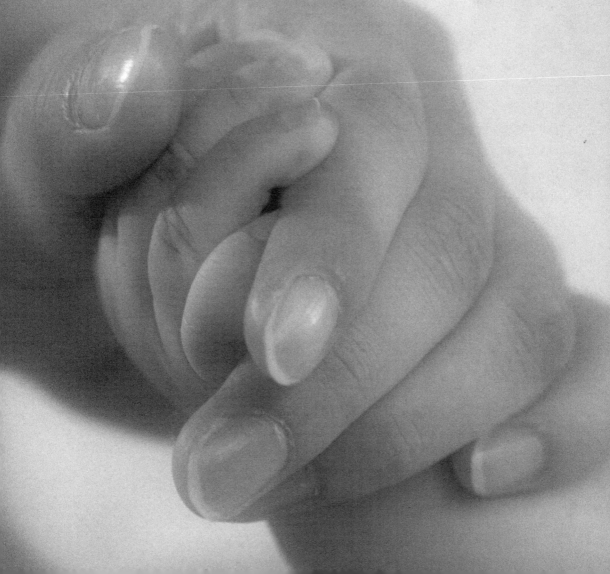

Health Check

Think back to a time when you were ill with not just a cold but something that kept you home from school. Maybe you were in the hospital for a while. Do your best to remember; then answer the following questions:

How long were you ill?

How did you feel emotionally when you first became ill?

How did you feel during the worst of it?

How did you feel when you began to improve?

How did you feel once it was all over?

Usually when persons are sick, they have several kinds of needs. Name the most important person in meeting each of these needs for you when you were ill:

Physical needs _____

Homework or
   other school needs _____

Tender, loving
   care needs _____

Bright thoughts
   or encouragement _____

Cards or phone calls _____

Transportation _____

Check all that apply:

Did you . . .

__ pray?

__ think about God?

__ wonder why folks become ill?

__ wonder if religious people are supposed to become ill?

__ Wonder how God helps people who are ill?

How do you think friends should respond when someone is ill or hurt?

What should Christians expect of God when they are ill?

Bible Study: Mark 2:1-12

Retell this story from the point of view of the various people in each of the four scenes in this section. The questions can help you. Use them, but don't let them limit you. Use your imagination.

Scene 1 (Verses 1-4)
The Friends

How did you hear about Jesus being in town?

___ One of us had seen Jesus.

___ A disciple told us.

___ Everyone knew, because Jesus stirred up controversy wherever he went.

How did you persuade the paralyzed man to "give it a try"?

___ We didn't ask; we just took him.

___ We took him but didn't tell him why.

___ We had been praying for his healing, and this seemed a natural next step.

When we carried him to where Jesus was preaching, we saw a crowd. We thought ...

___ This was a silly idea; why did we ever think of it?

___ How will we get through that many people?

___ Maybe we should have phoned ahead.

___ They won't let us through because they think that illness is a sign of sin.

___ We've come this far; there's no turning back now.

Tell this scene as one of the friends, including how you got the idea of dropping in on Jesus.

Scene 2 (Verses 4-5)
A Disciple Near Jesus

Jesus is standing next to you, preaching. A large crowd has gathered. What are you thinking?

___ This is amazing; wherever we go, it has been like this.

___ This man must be the Messiah.

___ I wonder what those scribes over in the corner are thinking.

___ This is too large of a crowd; something's bound to happen.

You begin to hear noises from the roof, and little bits of dirt and grass from the ceiling begin to fall on you and Jesus. What is your first thought?

___ The roof is caving in; Jesus will be hurt.

___ Let's get out of here!

___ The crowd is putting too much pressure on this small house; it's going to cave in any minute.

Then a large piece of the roof is lifted off from above, and you see four guys leaning over and looking into the room at Jesus. What are you tempted to do first?

__ Push Jesus out of the way to safety

__ Yell at the men to get down before they make the whole roof cave in

__ Complain at the men for their thoughtless interruption of Jesus' preaching

The men quickly lower a paralyzed friend into the room. You now clearly see that they want him healed. How do you feel?

__ Ashamed of yourself for being angry with them

__ Angry with them for interrupting Jesus' teaching?

__ Filled with compassion and admiring the creativity of the friends

Jesus turns to the paralytic and says, "Son, your sins are forgiven."

Tell this story as the disciple, including how you feel about those words being spoken to the man.

Scene 3 (Verses 5-11)
The Scribes

You have been wanting to hear what this new teacher has to say. When some guys lower a paralyzed man through the roof, what's your first thought?

__ These guys don't know the least thing about courtesy.

__ They must believe all those rumors they've heard about Jesus healing people.

__ Ah-*ha*! Now we can see what Jesus really can do.

Jesus turns to the paralyzed man and tells him that his sins are forgiven. Your deepest belief is that only God can forgive sin. Your reaction to those words is

__ A gasp of alarm. No man should dare claim to do what only God has the right to do.

__ A growl of anger. Who does he think he is?

__ A "hmm" of curiosity. This is a new twist, and it will be interesting to find out what Jesus means.

In spite of what Jesus has said, the paralyzed man is still where he is. You begin to think to yourself:

__ Maybe I misunderstood what he said.

__ Jesus truly can't heal.

__ The man came looking for healing. What does forgiveness of sins have to do with it?

Then Jesus looks you right in the eye. He seems to know what you've been thinking. He asks you which is easier to say—"Your sins are forgiven," or "Stand up and take up your mat and walk." Your answer, if he had given you time to make it, would have been:

___ I'd say forgiveness; no one could tell if I were right or wrong.

___ How dare you put me on the spot!

___ I'd say "Stand up and take up your mat"; even if it didn't work, it wouldn't get me in trouble with God.

Now tell this story as the scribe, including the order Jesus gives to the paralytic to take up his mat and go home.

Scene 4 (Verses 9-12)
Someone in the Crowd

Jesus is clearly about to have a run-in with the scribes, who you know are powerful. As the tension mounts, you find yourself thinking:

___ Who does Jesus think he is? These are our community's religious leaders.

___ Who do they think they are? Just because Jesus isn't a scribe, they want to find fault with him.

___ How does Jesus dare say things like that when they are here? Jesus is a good person, but he's gone overboard by thinking he can pronounce forgiveness.

Jesus seems to call himself "Son of Man." You know that phrase refers to someone who is supposed to be God's special person, one who is to bring in the kingdom of God. You begin to wonder:

___ Is this the end of the world?

___ Has Jesus gone off the deep end?

___ I'm afraid of him.

___ I'm afraid *for* him.

Jesus then turns to the paralyzed man and tells him to take up his mat and walk. In the split second before anything else happens, this thought races through your mind:

___ What if it doesn't work?

___ If it does work, what does that mean for me?

___ What if this is a trick?

___ What will the scribes do if the man does walk?

Now tell the story as a member of the crowd, including your reaction when the man in fact got up and walked.

Session *16*
The Disciples

A Dose of Realism

All around Jesus were rich and powerful people. Many of them felt threatened by what Jesus taught. Jesus had had some wonderful times with his disciples, but he knew there were difficult days ahead.

Jesus told his disciples what to expect. They needed to know the truth about what lay in store for them. But he also reminded them of God's promises.

Read each of the Scriptures in the Bible Study to see what Jesus expected to happen to his followers and how he encouraged them to remain faithful.

Bible Study: Matthew 10:16-23

Jesus put warnings and promises side by side. He said he was sending his disciples out like "sheep into the midst of wolves." What did he mean?

Verse 17-18 tells about three things Jesus expected his disciples would experience if they followed him. What are they?

In verses 19-20, Jesus tells his disciples how to behave when they get into trouble for preaching. What does he promise them?

Would the promise have eased your fears if you were they? Why, or why not?

In verses 21-22, what bad time does Jesus say the disciples may have to endure?

What is Jesus' promise to them?

Verse 23 again describes a problem the disciples may face and a promise Jesus makes.
ↂ The problem is
ↂ The promise is

Matthew 10:26-33

Jesus told his disciples not to fear and not to keep quiet. He told them to preach his message out in the light and to shout it from the housetops. What in these verses tells you he didn't think such a role was going to be easy?

Verses 29-31 contain two sayings. They were spoken to people who were in for a hard time. What do you think they mean?

In verse 32, Jesus makes a promise to those who are faithful: He will speak on their behalf before God. How, do you think, do the disciples feel about that promise?

Would that promise be enough to get you to face the same threats as they did? Why, or why not?

Mark 8:34-9:1

Again, Jesus told his disciples about the hard times they will face. Read the passage in the Bible. Then read this paraphrase:

> The disciples were there with a large crowd. Jesus called out loudly: "If you want to be my followers, forget about yourself, accept your responsibilities, and do what I do. When all you care about is yourself, you don't have a life; you've lost it without even knowing it. But if you try to bring good news to people and show them what it means to be a Christian—even if you get into trouble—you'll know that God and I are there with you. What good is it to pile up a lot of stuff if it costs you your closeness to God? Isn't your life worth more than a pile of junk, even if it's expensive junk? Some day God will complete the kingdom that God is starting here; when that happens, do you want to have to say to God that you were ashamed of me? Then I'll be ashamed of you."
>
> Then Jesus shouted to the crowd, 'This is the truth: While some of you are still living, you will see that God has come here with power."

If you were in the crowd hearing these words for the first time, what would your reaction be?

If you were a disciple, which verses would give you encouragement?

Say It Now

Rewrite the Bible verses below in today's language.

Be creative. For example, Matthew 10:27 ("What you hear whispered, proclaim from the housetops") could be rewritten as:

- If you believe in me, speak out!
- Don't keep me a secret—turn up the volume!
- Don't whisper—broadcast the good news!
- Don't hide my message on little scraps in your pocket; put it on a giant billboard!

Now you try your hand at these:

"See, I am sending you out like sheep into the midst of wolves."

"Let them deny themselves and take up their cross and follow me"

"Do not fear those who kill the body but cannot kill the soul."

"So do not be afraid; you are of more value than many sparrows."

Session 17
Peter's Confession

Who Do They Think You Are?

Below is a list of people you know. The question is, How well do they know you? When they think of you, do they capture the real you?

Write a word or phrase that best describes how you think each one thinks of you. For example, when the school principal hears your name, he or she probably thinks, *well behaved*. Your kid sister probably thinks, *fun—sometimes, at least*. Fill in the blanks with your first response.

Your best friend _____

The people you work for _____

Your worst enemy _____

Your mother _____

Your favorite teacher _____

Your father _____

Your least favorite teacher _____

Friends you see only at school _____

Your nearest neighbor _____

Your girlfriend or boyfriend _____

Your pastor _____

Your coach or band director _____

Your oldest brother or sister _____

Your grandparents _____

Your youngest brother or sister _____

Your doctor _____

Your school principal _____

Your youth group leaders _____

The adults in your church _____

Now go through the list and circle the three you believe best describe you.

Even the best descriptions leave something out. What would need to be added here to present a truer picture of you?

What is one way your own idea about who you are has changed in the last two years? (What is something you used to think about yourself that is no longer the case?)

Bible Study: Mark 8:27-33

Mix and Match

Match the following people from this passage to the definitions below. Place the number of the name in the blank by the correct definition.

1. John the Baptist
2. Elijah
3. prophets

4. Peter
5. Christ
6. Son of Man

7. elders
8. chief priests
9. scribes
10. Satan

__ One of the first disciples. His name also means "rock."

__ Not clergy or priests but still active leaders in the Jewish religion

__ A fiery preacher who baptized Jesus; some thought he might return from the dead to announce the arrival of the Messiah.

__ A name for a person some Jews expected to bring God's kingdom to earth

__ Professional teachers of the Jewish law

__ The name of a being that Jews believed tempted people to sin

__ An Old Testament prophet who many thought would return to earth to announce the dawn of God's kingdom

__ The professional religious leaders of the Jewish Temple

__ A word that also means "Messiah" and refers to a person whom Jews expected to restore Jewish rule to the nation of Israel

__ People who preached about God, calling the Jews to be faithful and to practice justice

Getting the Answers Right
Mark 8:27-30

Jesus had been preaching and healing people for quite a while. Now he was heading for Jerusalem on what would turn out to be his last trip. He asked his disciples, "Who do people say that I am?" What do his disciples answer in verse 28?

Considering that answer (and the definitions from "Mix and Match"), do you think that people understood who Jesus was? Why, or why not?

Jesus next asks Peter who he thinks Jesus is (verse 29). What is Peter's answer?

What do you think of Peter's answer?

Jesus tells the disciples not to tell anyone about him. Which of these statements helps explain why? *(You may check more than one.)*

__ Peter was wrong.

__ Peter was right, but others wouldn't understand.

__ The leaders would become upset if word got out that people thought Jesus was the Christ.

__ To the Jews, *Christ* meant someone who would defeat their enemies and set up an independent Jewish nation. If the Romans caught wind of that speculation, there would be trouble for everyone.

Getting the Answers Wrong
Mark 8:31-33

In the Jewish belief, the Son of Man was one who would come in power and victory to bring God's kingdom. Jesus had a different idea about what would happen to the Son of Man. What was it?

How did Peter respond?

Judging from Peter's response, do you think he truly understood who Jesus was? Why, or why not?

Thought Question

Peter thought that Christ would come with power and should not suffer. Jesus, however, thought that to be on the side of God, he needed to suffer rather than take over the nation with power.

Jesus, therefore, called Peter "Satan," the one who tempts a person to sin. Do you think that Jesus was tempted to become the kind of Christ that Peter expected?

In verse 33, Jesus speaks harshly to Peter, calling him Satan and telling him to get away from him. What did Peter done that was so dangerous?

My Creed

A creed is a statement telling what you believe. In fact, *creed* comes from the word *credo,* which means "I believe." In the space below, state your belief about Jesus. Write what you truly believe at this point in your life.

As you come to know Jesus more and grow in your faith, you may deepen or even change some beliefs you hold now. That progression is to be expected. At a later time, write a new creed for yourself. If you save this page, put today's date on it, and reread it at that time, you will have a way of seeing how you are growing spiritually.

I believe that Jesus is

Session 18
The Transfiguration

You're So Much Like . . .

Listed below are several people. Most of them probably know you quite well. Who in your family would they be most likely to say you are like? If they already have someone they think you are similar to, write that name down. If not, try to imagine who they might say you are most like.

Your mother? _____

Your sister? _____

Your father? _____

Your brother? _____

Your grandmother? _____

The aunt you know best? _____

Your grandfather? _____

The uncle you know best? _____

Which of them, in your opinion, comes closest to being right? _____

In what ways?

Uncovered!

Imagine that a sudden sandstorm filled your neighborhood with sand and that your room was preserved exactly as it sits right now. A team of teenage archeologists uncover it a thousand years from now. What would they learn about you? What interests would they find you had? What evidence of your belief in God would they find? What else would they learn about you?

Bible Study: Mark 9:2-8

This episode is called The Transfiguration. The word has two parts: *figuration,* which means "to give a shape to something" (and referred at first to making something out of clay, the way a potter does); and *trans,* which means "across." So, *transfiguration* means "to put a new shape to something right across its old shape."

In this story, the transfiguration happens to Jesus; he doesn't exactly change his shape, but his appearance changes in an unusual way.

1. Jesus took with him _____ and _____ and _____.

2. He led them up a high _____ apart, by themselves.

3. When he was transfigured, his _____ became dazzling white.

4. And there appeared to them _____ and _____, who were talking with Jesus.

5. When Peter saw what was happening, what did he offer to do?

6. A cloud overshadowed them, and from the cloud there came a voice, saying:

7. Then what happened?

8. What do these Old Testament passages have in common with the story of the Transfiguration?

✐ Exodus 24:1-2

✐ Exodus 24:15-18

✐ Exodus 34:29-30

9. **What do we know about the burial places of Moses and Elijah? They have something in common. (Look at 2 Kings 2:11 and Deuteronomy 34:6.)**

10. **Read Malachi 4:4-6. (Malachi is the last book in the Old Testament.) What special meaning did Elijah have for Israel?**

Christians Transformed

In **2 Corinthians 3:7-18,** Paul compares the shining experiences of Moses and Jesus. Moses' face was so bright from being with God he had to wear a veil so that people could look at him. Paul claims that the glory of Jesus is far greater. The word of hope for us is that as we set our hearts and minds on Jesus and live in his presence, we are being transformed ourselves into the image of Christ.

Thought Question

If you were Mark, what meaning would you hope your readers would get from these parts of your story of Jesus' Transfiguration?

⍟ The event took place on a mountain.

⍟ Three men accompanied Jesus.

⍟ Jesus' appearance was dazzling.

⍟ Moses was there.

⍟ Elijah was there.

⍟ Peter wanted to make three dwellings (booths or tents used in a Jewish festival that celebrated God's act of salvation in the Exodus).

⍟ A cloud came over them, and God's voice spoke.

Session 19
I Am ...

Who Is Jesus?

In the Gospel of John, Jesus speaks about who he is. Seven of those speeches include the "I am" sayings. In each one, Jesus describes himself a little differently, but taken all together, the images give us a greater sense of who Jesus is.

Match the images below to the correct Bible verses. Draw a line connecting the pair.

Images	Bible Passages
Bread of life	John 15:1
Light of the world	John 14:6
Gate (door)	John 11:25
Good Shepherd	John 6:35
Resurrection and life	John 8:12
Way, truth, and life	John 10:14
True vine	John 10:9

Choose Only Two

Suppose you were the writer of the Gospel of John. Suppose, further, that you didn't have room to include in your Gospel all of the "I Am" statements. In fact, you could use only two of them. Which two would you choose?

> Here are some thoughts to help you make your decision: Which images are the most memorable? Which ones seem to say the most? Which one do most people need to hear most often? Which of those images of Jesus speaks best to you?

1.

2.

Tell why you chose those two.

Bible Study

Jesus the Light
John 8:12-20

◊ In verse 12, what does Jesus promise to those who follow him?

◊ In verse 13, the Pharisees criticize Jesus. What do they say?

◊ Read verses 14, 17, and 18. Jesus claims that he does have a second witness to who he is. Who is that witness?

◊ Had the Pharisees known the other "witness," do you think they would have known who Jesus was? Why, or why not?

◊ Jesus told the Pharisees that he was the light of the world. Do you think the Pharisees "saw the light"? Why, or why not?

Light at the Feast

The Feast of Tabernacles helped the Jews remember the time when they wandered in the wilderness, guided through the night by the light of a flaming pillar. The Jews later began to use the image of "light" to describe things that guided them in other ways. For example, the Law, which guided them in their religion, was sometimes called an undying light.

At the ceremonies for the Feast of Tabernacles, on the first night, four large golden candlesticks were lighted. The candlesticks were in bowls set so high that someone had to climb up a ladder to light them. The light given by those huge candles was said to be so bright that it lighted up much of Jerusalem.

Scholars believe that Jesus was standing in the very courtyard where those candles were lit when he described himself as the light of the world. If so, Jesus was describing himself as a light even greater than the light for the Tabernacle Feast. That light illuminated only Jerusalem. Jesus' light was for the whole world.

Why, do you think, did Jesus choose to speak of light while standing in that place? Can you understand why the Pharisees were upset with him?

Jesus the Gate
John 10:1-10

✐ In verses 1 and 2, Jesus describes two kinds of people who have interest in sheep:

✐ According to verses 3 and 4, how does the shepherd relate to his sheep? How does he care for them?

✐ How will the sheep respond to the stranger?

✐ In verses 9 and 10, Jesus describes what waits for those who see that he is the gate. What does he say?

✐ If Jesus calls himself the gate, what do the religious leaders who disagreed with him represent?

✐ Do you think the Pharisees regarded Jesus as the gateway to God? Why, or why not?

✐ If the Pharisees were to choose an image for Jesus, what image might they choose?

✐ What would they want that image to tell others about Jesus?

Sheep and the Gate

Some translations refer to the gate in this passage as a door. The sheep were kept inside the penned-in area unless the gatekeeper let them out. The gate and gatekeeper protected the sheep from thieves.

During the years leading up to Jesus' time, several men had become high priests and Temple leaders who were, in fact, discovered to be thieves. Those leaders, who were supposed to be the shepherds of the people, were instead stealing from them.

Jesus often referred to his followers as his "little flock." In his arguments with the Pharisees and priests, he tried to protect the people from them. When he did so, he was like the gate that kept the thieves out and let in only those who truly cared for the people.

Read further in **John 10** to find out more about Jesus and his "sheep."

Session 20
Palm Sunday

How Would You Tell?

Rumors are flying like crazy: People think the Messiah has returned! You have been put on a panel of experts to investigate this person. You represent the Christian church and must bring a Christian point of view to the committee.

Twenty centuries have passed since Jesus came. If the person who has come in our time is the Messiah, you believe he would have to be like Jesus.

If you saw this new person, how would you tell whether he was the Messiah? What would you expect him to be like?

How would you expect the Messiah to be dressed? (*Check one.*)
__ a three-piece suit
__ jeans
__ like a Jewish shepherd
__ no one would notice

What language would the Messiah speak?
__ Aramaic (the language Jesus spoke)
__ English
__ Spanish
__ all languages

What mode of transportation would he use?
__ donkey
__ limo
__ personal jet
__ he would just appear

How would he speak to world leaders?
__ angrily
__ sympathetically
__ helpfully
__ sadly

What would his attitude be toward each of the following groups of people?

The poor _____

Women _____

The rich _____

Children _____

The sick _____

The homeless _____

The Christian church _____

Other religions _____

Would he be primarily a (*check one*)
__ preacher
__ teacher
__ homeless person
__ government leader
__ celebrity
__ military leader
__ social worker

Which of these groups of people would you expect to be among his closest friends?
(*Check as many as you need to.*)
__ revolutionary leaders
__ business owners
__ mayors and senators
__ pastors
__ high school students
__ single people
__ musicians
__ movie stars
__ teachers
__ farmers
__ owners of large businesses
__ accountants and workers from the Internal Revenue Service
__ intellectuals
__ famous writers
__ doctors
__ athletes

Which characteristic of Jesus would you most look for as you examine this person?

Why did you select that characteristic?

Bible Study: Old Testament

In Jesus' time, many people had an idea of what the Messiah would be like. Their expectations came in part from the Hebrew Scriptures (the Old Testament).

Zechariah 9:9-10. From this passage what would you say the Jews expected of the Messiah?

ᴓ His attitude:

ᴓ His transportation:

ᴓ What he would do about war:

ᴓ How extensive his rule would be:

2 Kings 9:11-13. In this story, Elisha had sent a prophet to bring a message to Jehu. Jehu has just received the message from the prophet, has come out from his room, and has been greeted by his servants.

ᴓ What is the message Jehu has received?

ᴓ How do his servants respond?

Psalm 68:24-25. When the new king came, the Jews expected a parade like the one described here.

ᴓ Where is the procession going?

ᴓ Who is in the procession?

> ## Patriotic Psalms
> The Jews longed for the coming of the Messiah, whom they expected would be a great king like David. He would start a revolution, drive out the Romans, and set up a Jewish kingdom, with Jerusalem as its capital. Passover was a festival of freedom, so patriotic feelings were especially high. The psalms sung for "going up to Jerusalem" were patriotic songs.

Psalm 118:25-27. People watching the procession might shout, "Save us!" What's another way of saying that phrase?

___ Maranatha!
___ For heaven's sake!
___ Hosanna!

ᴓ On whom does verse 26 shout a blessing?

ᴓ What in verse 27 might make Christians think of Palm Sunday?

Bible Study: Mark 11:1-11

Jesus Approaches Jerusalem

Jesus is preparing to go into Jerusalem. He has already told his friends that he expects to suffer and perhaps die there.

On the way, Jesus gives an assignment to two disciples. What is it?

What are the disciples to say if they are questioned?

How does Jesus refer to himself?

Match the Old Testament passages from the first Bible study in this session with what happened in Mark:

Verse 7. _____

Verse 8. _____

Verse 9. _____

Verse 10. _____

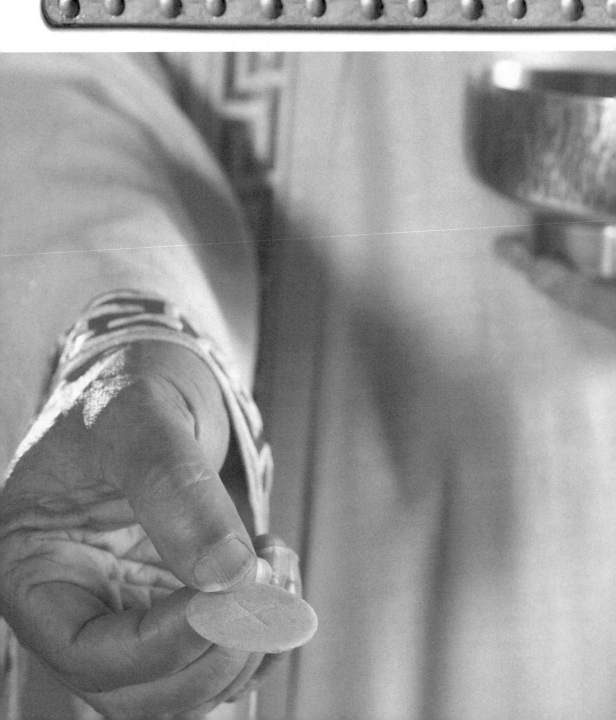

Session 21
The Last Supper

Certainties

Rate each of the sentences below to show how certain you are of its truth. Circle the number that best expresses how you truly feel about the statement to its left—not how you think you should feel. You will not have to show this page to others unless you wish to do so.

1 = I am absolutely certain.
2 = I am reasonably certain.
3 = I am not quite sure.
4 = I find this really hard to believe.

1. God loves me.	1	2	3	4
2. I love God.	1	2	3	4
3. God trusts me.	1	2	3	4
4. I trust God.	1	2	3	4
5. Christ believes in me.	1	2	3	4
6. I believe in Christ.	1	2	3	4
7. Jesus fulfilled his mission on earth.	1	2	3	4
8. I can fulfill my mission on earth.	1	2	3	4
9. Jesus loved others.	1	2	3	4
10. I love others.	1	2	3	4
11. The church cares for me.	1	2	3	4
12. I care for the church.	1	2	3	4
13. The church is good for me.	1	2	3	4
14. I am good for the church.	1	2	3	4
15. Jesus did what is right.	1	2	3	4
16. I will do what is right.	1	2	3	4
17. Jesus kept his faith even in danger.	1	2	3	4
18. I will keep my faith even in danger.	1	2	3	4
19. Jesus knew what he believed.	1	2	3	4
20. I know what I believe.	1	2	3	4
21. True disciples never doubt God.	1	2	3	4
22. True disciples never doubt themselves.	1	2	3	4
23. Jesus loves even those who fail him.	1	2	3	4
24. Jesus doesn't expect us to be certain, only faithful.	1	2	3	4
25. God strengthens us to serve Christ better.	1	2	3	4

Thought Questions

In your opinion, how confident were the disciples in Jesus as a man? ___ in their faith in Jesus as God's son? ___ *(Place one of the numbers from the previous page in each of the blanks.)*

Tell why you answered the way you did. What examples or stories from the New Testament help explain your answers?

What experiences from your life help explain your answers?

Bible Study:
Matthew 26:17-30

The Scripture verses for today tell about Jesus' last supper with his friends. We remember this meal every time the church celebrates Holy Communion.

Read Matthew 26:17-30 aloud. If you are in a group, assign one person to read the words Jesus speaks, one to read the words spoken by Judas, and one person to be the narrator (to read all of the lines that are not in quotation marks). When there are lines spoken by all of the disciples, everyone should speak them.

Jesus spoke of eating the Passover. What is Passover?

Jesus instructed his disciples to go into the city and tell a certain man, "My time is near." What could that statement mean?

In your opinion, how could Jesus have known that someone in Jerusalem would let him and his disciples use his house?

Pretend that you are one of the disciples, not Judas, and that you heard Jesus say, "Truly I tell you, one of you will betray me." What would your first reaction be?

How did the disciples react?

Why, do you think, did all of the disciples ask, "Surely not I, Lord?"

Judas had betrayed Jesus. When Jesus said that it would be better for his betrayer never to have been born, how do you think Judas felt?

Judas had been with Jesus throughout Jesus' ministry. Do you think Judas truly believed what Jesus had been saying about himself and about the kingdom of God? Why, or why not?

When Judas said, "Surely not I, Rabbi?" Jesus answered, "You have said so." What did Jesus mean by that comment?

All of the disciples have just announced their uncertainty—they did not know whether they would betray Jesus. In spite of that announcement, Jesus went ahead and shared a meal with them. Why, in your opinion, would anyone do so?

When Jesus took bread, blessed it, and gave it to his disciples, what familiar words did he speak?

What do you think Jesus is telling his friends to expect?

Which of the following statements means the most to you concerning Jesus' statement about the bread?

___ Whenever you eat bread, I want you to remember what it was like when I was with you.

___ God gave bread to feed the children of Israel in the wilderness; now he gives me to feed your spirit at all times.

___ Bread is the source of life; and I am the source of the courage you will need to live after I am gone.

___ Other:

When he pours wine, he calls it "my blood of the covenant." A covenant is an agreement between God and people. Which of these statements about the new covenant mean the most to you when you participate in Holy Communion?

___ God's love will reach out to all people and not only the Jews.

___ God will continue to seek out sinners and forgive them.

___ Disciples will find the strength and love they need to carry out God's work.

___ Other:

Passover

This spring festival of freedom commemorates the Exodus of the Hebrews from Egypt. It is called Passover because God said to the Hebrews, "I will pass over you, and no plague shall destroy you when I strike the land of Egypt" (**Exodus 12:13b**). The plague took the lives of the first-born children in the households of the Egyptians but passed over the first-born of the Hebrews.

Passover is also called the Feast of Unleavened Bread, because the Hebrews, when escaping from Egypt, did not have time to put leaven, or yeast, in their bread to make it rise. Jewish families also eat lamb for the Passover meal. Lamb's blood marked the homes of the Hebrews in Egypt so that the angel of death would pass over them. When Jesus celebrated Passover with his friends at his last supper, he gave the meal a new meaning.

Many people expected that if God's kingdom were to come, it would come during Passover and especially on Passover night. The followers of the risen Christ, however, believed that God had begun the Kingdom in Jesus. They continued to share the Passover meal but used it to remember how God had freed them from sin and death, rather than to celebrate being freed from Egypt.

Christians today continue to share in Passover every time we have Holy Communion. But now we participate in the Lord's Supper to remember Jesus and to give thanks to God for forgiveness and for new strength to be faithful disciples.

Session 22
The Trial and Crucifixion

Bible Study: Mark 15:1-41

Fateful Threes

In Mark 15:1, three kinds of people meet with the council to decide what to do with Jesus. What were they?

_____ _____ _____

Three times Pilate uses the phrase "King of the Jews." In what verses does he use the phrase, and to whom is he speaking each time?

1. _____ _____

2. _____ _____

3. _____ _____

In verses 6-15, three men are mentioned by name. Who are they, and what are they?

1. _____ _____

2. _____ _____

3. _____ _____

Pilate asks the crowd three questions. What are they, and how does the crowd answer?

Question 1

Answer

Question 2

Answer

Question 3

Answer

Three more times in verses 16-32 Jesus is called king. What are the verses, and what is he called king of in each?

1. _____ _____

2. _____ _____

3. _____ _____

In verse 19, Jesus is in the hands of the soldiers. What three things do they do to him?

1.

2.

3.

How many men were crucified, and who were they?

After Jesus was crucified (verse 27), three kinds of people mocked him. Who were they, and what did they say?

1. _____   _____

2. _____   _____

3. _____   _____

In verse 34, Jesus cries out to God. People standing by make three responses. In which verses do those responses occur, and what do they say?

1. _____   _____

2. _____   _____

3. _____   _____

Three women watch the entire event from afar. Who are they?

_____   _____   _____

The events in this Bible study begin in the morning (verse 1) and end in the evening (verse 42). Between morning and evening, Mark has three references to time. What are they, and what happens at each of them?

1. _____   _____

2. _____   _____

3. _____   _____

Do you notice anything unusual about those three numbers? If so, what is it?

The End

Scene 1: In Pilate's Garden

READER A: Pilate was the Roman governor of Judea from 26–36 A.D. His headquarters were in Caesarea. He was responsible for keeping order in Israel. He used the Roman army to help him keep the nation under control. That army was the mightiest in the world, and the people of Israel had no hope of overcoming it.

Pilate had a reputation for being merciless and cruel. He most likely mocked his victims to remind them of how helpless they were. He was accustomed to have people obey him and to answer his questions.

Yet, after answering only one of Pilate's questions, Jesus chose to stay silent before him. I wonder why.

READER B: (*Read Mark 15:1-5.*)

Scene 2: In Front of the Crowd by the Courtyard
(*Move to a new location in the room.*)

READER C: If it weren't for Jesus, no one today would know of Barabbas. His name is interesting. The first part, *bar,* means "son." The second part, *abba,* means "father." Jesus called God "Abba"—his Father. Barabbas's name, then, means "son of the father." He stood before Jesus not knowing that Jesus was the true Son of the Father, who is in heaven.

Pilate placed the two men, Jesus and Barabbas, before the crowd and promised to release whichever one the crowd chose. It didn't take the crowd long to make its decision. After all, Barabbas was a man who had tried to free the Jews. Jesus was just a rabbi—a troublesome one at that, according to the religious powers of the day, stirring up the crowd. The people called for Barabbas.

Jesus didn't protest. He did not wish to see others' blood shed. As he had said at his Last Supper, he would pour out his blood for many people. Why didn't he repeat that statement to Pilate, or to Barabbas? I wonder.

READER D: (*Read Mark 15:6-15.*)

Scene 3: Inside the Palace
(*Move to a new location in the room.*)

READER E: The soldiers who took Jesus to prepare him for crucifixion abused him. They also made fun of him, pretending to treat him as if he were a king.

Kings wore robes of expensive fabrics dyed in deep purple. The soldiers put one of their own rough red cloaks on Jesus, as a mockery of an emperor's robe.

The Roman emperor wore a wreath of laurel, a beautiful vine awarded to victors in battle and in athletics. The soldiers placed not laurel but a wreath of thorns on Jesus.

The Romans greeted their emperor with the shout, "Hail Caesar, Victor and Leader." They sneered at Jesus, saluting him and saying, "Hail, King of the Jews."

They dressed him like a shabby emperor and called him king to mock him. Didn't any of them know who he was? I wonder.

READER F: (*Read Mark 15:16.*)

Scene 4: At Golgotha
(*Move to a new location in the room.*)

READER G: A condemned man was expected to carry the crossbeam of his cross to the place where he was to be crucified. In Jerusalem, the place of crucifixion was Golgotha, which means "the place of the skull." The hill itself was nearly skull-shaped, and the skulls of many people had hung in death there.

It was customary to give a dying man on the cross something to ease his pain. They offered Jesus wine, and later vinegar; he did not take either.

Death on a cross was not quick and simple, and it was not pretty. The victim's arms were either tied or nailed to the cross piece. The crosspiece was then attached to a long, vertical post, like the crossbar on the letter T. The weight of the body rested on a small stake or bar. Victims often hung for days and died of hunger and thirst. Sometimes, to be merciful, soldiers would end the victims' lives by piercing them with spears or by breaking their legs.

Jesus accepted his dying without expressing hatred. They mocked him, yet he acted with the dignity of a true king. Why didn't the soldiers and passersby notice that virtue? I wonder.

READER H: (*Read Mark 15:21-32.*)

Scene 5: Close to the Cross
(*Move to a new place, and stand close together.*)

READER I: Many Jews believed that the prophet Elijah would return to aid the people in time of need. Jesus' cry from the cross sounded so much like Elijah's name that some people thought he must have been calling out for Elijah to deliver him.

Some Jews had thought that Jesus might be that old prophet himself. Do you remember what the disciples said when Jesus asked them, "Who do men say that I am?" One answer was Elijah.

Jesus' cry would also remind Jews of a prayer from the Old Testament. Psalm 22 begins with these words:

My God, My God, why have you forsaken me?
  Why are you so far from helping me, from the words of my groaning?

Was Jesus thinking of those words? Was he praying that old prayer? If so, was he feeling the deep sadness expressed in the prayer? Or did he also pray the rest of the prayer, the part that says that God "did not despise . . . the affliction of the afflicted; he did not hide his face from me, but heard when I cried to him" (verse 24)?

Was Jesus calling Elijah? Was he praying the prayer of sadness? Was he praying the prayer of one who knew that God had heard when he cried to him, or did he feel forsaken? I wonder.

READER J: *(Read Mark 15:33-38.)*

Session 23
Resurrection!

What Would You Do?

It is early Sunday morning. You have been awake most of the night. Your close friend, Jesus of Nazareth, was crucified two days ago.

On that night, just as it was turning dark, a man named Joseph had taken Jesus from the cross and placed him in a tomb. He sealed the tomb with a huge stone to protect it until after the holy day (Saturday).

You have followed everything closely. The other friends of Jesus ran away when he was arrested. You have not seen them since. Only you and two others remain now. The time since the Crucifixion has been difficult. No one knows if Jesus' followers will also be arrested. Going out in public feels dangerous.

So you have waited, worried, and grieved. And you've told stories about Jesus to cheer up the others and yourself. Mostly, you just kept going until the Sabbath passed. Today, the first day of the week, you and your two friends have bought some spices. Now is the time to properly care for the body.

You head for the burial place talking quietly, hoping someone will be there to help you remove the stone and allow the three of you to enter the tomb.

Read **Mark 16:1-8.**

Who are you?

_____, _____, and _____

What did you see?

Whom did you see?

What did you hear?

What did you do?

Tell why, using your imagination.

If It Happened to You . . .

Suppose that the Resurrection just happened this morning, and you were one of the three people who discovered it. All of the others have gone. You and your friends are not considered leaders of the group. But you are the only ones who have heard the word, and you haven't heard it from Jesus but from a stranger standing by his tomb.

So now, in your century and time . . .

Would you tell? Why, or why not?

Whom would you tell?

Who do you think would believe you?

What would you expect them to do?

Thought Questions

If you were the women, would you tell others what you saw and heard? Why, or why not?

Whom would you tell?

Who do you think would believe you?

What would you expect them to do?

Bible Study: Mark 14–15

Mark 14:43-50. This scene takes place in the Garden of Gethsemane on the night that Jesus was arrested. Three actions are taken by the disciples, two by individuals, and one by the group. The actions occur in verses 43-45, verse 47, and verse 50. What are they?

1. The disciples . . .

2. Two individuals . . .

3. The group . . .

If these actions were all you knew of the disciples, what would your opinion of them be?

Mark 14:66-72. After Jesus was arrested and his friends ran away, Peter hovered nearby for a while. He had told Jesus that he would never deny him. What happened?

If this action were all you knew about Peter, what would your opinion of him be?

Tell briefly who the main characters are in each of these passages and what they do:

◊ Mark 15:39

◊ Mark 15:46-47

◊ Mark 16:1-2

Who's True?

In the closing chapters of his Gospel, Mark has shown that the men who followed Jesus closely as disciples nevertheless deny him. But Mark also shows

◊ an enemy soldier (the centurion) recognizing Jesus on the cross as the Son of God;

◊ a Jewish leader (Joseph of Arimathea) caring for his body;

◊ the women followers as the only ones who remained close to Jesus through it all. When Jesus rises from the dead, the women are the first to get the message.

If these details were all you knew about the story, who would you consider to be the true disciples?

Resurrectable Secrets

The women came to the tomb. They found the tomb empty, but the person at the tomb filled their minds with an exciting new idea: Jesus was risen!

But the women were afraid—with good reason. Jesus had been killed for saying the things he did. Would they be killed too? How were they supposed to share this good news? Most men in that day didn't care what women said. Would anyone believe them with such a fantastic story? Like the women, you have good news and, probably, some reservations about sharing it with your friends.

However, most people see faith in others not just by what they say but also in what they do, how they treat others, and the attitude with which they approach things. What are some ways you can share that you are a Christian without "preaching" to your friends?

Do you have a talent or interest that would show your love for God and others? Is there something you would like to be asked to do at your church but would never volunteer to do? Are you afraid that people might laugh at you if you tried doing this task? What would happen if you got the courage to do that thing? What if someone asked you to demonstrate that talent?

Think of some things you can do but are reluctant to do in front of others or have never had the opportunity to do. List two or three of them here:

Of the things listed above, choose the one you believe might best be used for serving God and others:

Think now about those women. How would the world—and your life—be different if they had never found the courage to tell the good news? What if no one ever knew that Jesus was the Messiah, the one who lives eternally?

What are a few ways you can use that particular talent or interest to show your love for God?

What commitment are you willing to make to God about using your talent or interest for God?

Choose a date by which you commit to use your talent.

Session 24
Jesus and Thomas

What Would You Believe?

People believe a lot of different things. Some seem pretty silly. Members of the Flat Earth Society, for example, believe that our planet is nearly flat, like the top of a Frisbee. If you go too far, they say, you might fall right over the edge.

Other beliefs are quite important. Take, for example, the belief that truth is better than falsehood. No one can put that belief in a test tube and prove it. But what would life be like if we didn't believe it and act according to it? You would never be able to trust anybody.

One difference between unimportant beliefs and important ones is that we can usually give some good reasons for the good ones. We can point to something like the belief's importance in living a good life or in keeping society healthy or in caring for others.

You can usually tell a belief is far fetched when you ask a person why he or she believes it and the answer you get is, "I just do; that's all there is to it," or "I don't know; it's just how I feel."

Mark the statements below that you believe:

__ 1. Other planets have intelligent life there.

__ 2. Angels exist.

__ 3. Some fish are so small that they can't see themselves.

__ 4. In every atom there is a world like ours, and our world is just an atom of a much larger one.

__ 5. Democracy is better than socialism.

__ 6. Wars are necessary to keep the population down.

__ 7. Peter Pan was a real boy.

__ 8. Money is the best reason for selecting a career.

__ 9. No one has to be poor; everyone can succeed with enough effort.

__ 10. Teens today know more than their parents did when they were teens.

__ 11. We use only ten percent of our mental powers.

__ 12. Spoiled meat will turn into maggots.

__ 13. Sports cars are better than station wagons.

__ 14. "Made in America" means made better.

__ 15. America is the greatest country.

__ 16. Advertising is mostly truthful.

__ 17. Dogs can talk to each other in their own form of language.

__ 18. People who are smart have better morals.

__ 19. Christians are usually nicer than non-Christians.

__ 20. The most important thing to study in school is science.

__ 21. Pigs are smarter than horses.

__ 22. Lightning bugs are born during thunderstorms.

__ 23. People all over the world are pretty much the same, and they would get along just fine if their leaders didn't interfere.

__ 24. People who take a lot of vitamins stay healthy longer.

__ 25. High school is the most important time of your life.

Now go through the list again. This time, pick out one sentence that you believe quite strongly is true, write its number here _____, and give some reasons you believe it.

Go through the list one more time, selecting one sentence that you think is really far fetched. Write its number here _____, and give some reasons you do not believe it.

Bible Study: John 20:19-29

Scene 1 (Verses 19-23). After Jesus' resurrection, he appears to several of his disciples. Only one feature of the room is mentioned in the story.

ø What is it?

ø Why, do you think, did John choose to mention that feature?

ø Jesus says, "Peace be with you." Then he shows them something. What, and why?

ø Only after that demonstration does the Bible say the disciples were glad to see Jesus. What might they have been feeling when he first appeared?

ø In verses 22-23, Jesus breathes on the disciples. Genesis says that God's breath breathed life into the first human. What new life and power was Jesus breathing into the first disciples?

Scene 2 (Verses 24-25). Thomas was absent when Jesus visited the other disciples. His friends give him their good news.

ø What is his reaction?

ø In your opinion, which of these words best describes Thomas's attitude? (check one)

__ foolish
__ reasonable
__ unfaithful
__ doubtful
__ unreasonable
__ scientific

ø Jesus tells Thomas, "Blessed are those who have not seen and yet have come to believe." How does that teaching apply to Thomas?

✐ Did the other disciples believe Jesus without seeing him?

✐ Did Thomas want more evidence than the other disciples had, or less?

✐ Had you been in Thomas's place, what would your reaction have been?

Scene 3 (Verses 26-29). Eight days later, Jesus appears again. Compare verse 26 with verse 19.

✐ In what ways are they similar?

✐ What does Jesus offer to Thomas?

✐ What is Thomas's response to Jesus?

✐ Jesus tells Thomas, "Blessed are those who have not seen and yet have come to believe." How does that teaching apply to Thomas?

✐ Did the other disciples believe Jesus without seeing him?

Doubting "Doubting Thomas"
John 11:7-8, 14-16

Because he did not immediately believe that the disciples had seen Jesus, Thomas has been known as "Doubting Thomas." Do you think he was any more doubting or unbelieving than the other disciples? Why?

The story of the danger to Jesus (John 11:7-8, 14-16) gives us another picture of Thomas. If this scene were all we knew about Thomas, how do you think he would be known today? *(Check one.)*

   __ Loyal Thomas
   __ Brave Thomas
   __ Faithful Thomas
   __ Believing Thomas
   __ Doubting Thomas

In your opinion, why would a man as brave as Thomas hesitate to believe the disciples when they said that they had seen Jesus? *(Check as many as you agree with.)*

__ He loved Jesus so much that he didn't want to be fooled.

__ The disciples had been fearful, and he didn't know whether he could trust their report.

__ Like most action-oriented people, he would believe only what he had seen.

__ He knew how dangerous rumors and false beliefs could be.

__ Some of the other disciples (such as Peter, James, and John) had claimed to have special visions before (like the Transfiguration); and yet, when the pressure was on, they were cowards. That flaw would make any reasonable man doubt such reports from them.

Why Tell That Story?
John 20:29-31

John's Gospel was written at least sixty years after Jesus had died. Nearly all of the Christians who had known Jesus personally were dead. Keep that information in mind as you reread John 20:29-31.

John was writing his Gospel for people who had never seen Jesus. What problem might he have been facing with them?

Why, do you think, did he choose to tell them the story about Thomas?

In verse 30, John tells us Jesus said and did many things that are not included in the Gospel. So John selected stories that would accomplish a certain purpose. What was that purpose?

Do you think he should have added other kinds of things? If not, why? If so, what kinds of things would you have wanted him to include?

Session 25
The Road to Emmaus

Tell the Story

Have you ever noticed how much easier it is to tell a joke than to write one? or to tell a friend about your fabulous vacation than to write a paper about it for school? Some stories are just easier to communicate and to understand when they are told orally

Most of the stories about Jesus were told at first, not written. But print can't show us how a storyteller would gesture or smile or pause or turn a phrase.

Print can't do all of those things, but you can. You can get a story off that page, away from the eye, and give it back to the voices and the ears the way it originally was. Here are some tips for bringing the story to life:

1. **Read the entire story.**

2. **Find the parts of the story.** Most stories have four parts: an introduction, the problem or mystery or situation that has to be resolved by the characters, something that builds tension, and a solution.

3. **Imagine the story.** What do the people act like? How would they talk? What would they be feeling? What gestures would they make?

4. **Imagine yourself telling the story.** Close your eyes and listen for your voice in your head. Imagine how you would say the words. Try emphasizing different things.

5. **Practice it.**

Bible Study: The Emmaus Road

Part 1: Luke 24:13-21

Follow all of the tips in "Tell the Story" (above). Your part of the story introduces the scene and begins to set out the problem. Here are some facts to get you started:

1. The two men were walking.

2. It was the Sunday after Jesus was killed, so the memory and grief were still strong.

3. Jesus caught up with them from behind, and they didn't know who he was.

4. The men were surprised that the stranger could have been in Jerusalem without knowing what had happened to Jesus.

5. The disciples still referred to Jesus as a prophet mighty in word and deed. They had not learned that Jesus expected to suffer. They still expected the Messiah to be a military leader.

6. Jesus had been dead for three days, and they had lost hope.

Put yourself in their shoes, and tell the story.

Part 2: Luke 24:22-27

Follow all of the tips in "Tell the Story" (page 107). Your part of the story gives some clues about the solution, but the real outcome is not yet in sight. Here are some observations and questions to stir your imagination:

1. Part 1 ends with the two friends feeling hopeless and telling their sad story to a stranger (who is Jesus—but they don't know it).

2. The disciples now begin to tell the stranger about the women having visited the tomb, finding it empty, and getting a message from an angel that Jesus was alive. They waited quite a while before telling this story to the stranger. Were they embarrassed by something that seemed to be foolish? Did they believe that the story was only gossip and therefore feel worse about their loss? Were they simply puzzled by it all? Think about their mood.

3. Jesus speaks to them, calling them "foolish men." Think about how he does so. Is he angry? gentle? sympathetic?

4. Jesus begins to teach them. He reminds them that the Messiah was not to be a great military hero but one who suffered. As he teaches, does he speak impatiently? quickly? slowly? as though he were passing on a precious secret?

5. Jesus teaches them about himself without revealing who he is. How, do you think, would Jesus have kept the men from knowing who he was? If you were the storyteller, how would you show that?

Part 3: Luke 24:28-35

This part of the story brings the plot to its conclusion. Something special is revealed. Use the storytelling tips in "Tell the Story" (page 106) and the following ideas to help you tell your part of the story:

1. Jesus has been explaining the Scriptures, telling the men that the Messiah came to suffer, not to bring military victory.

2. They arrive at Emmaus, at the home of one of the men.

3. Jesus intends to go on. How do the men get him to stay and eat with them? How important to them is his doing so?

4. Jesus takes bread, gives thanks, and gives it to the men—exactly as he had done at the Last Supper. Can you make gestures showing the bread being broken, as though Communion were being served?

5. As the bread is being handed out, two things happen almost instantly: The men recognize Jesus, and he vanishes. How would you express that sudden turn of events?

6. Then the disciples each say what they had felt privately when Jesus taught them the Scriptures: "Were not our hearts burning within us ... while he was opening the Scriptures to us?" Each disciple discovered that the other felt the same way. How would they express that surprise?

7. They had great news to give to their friends in Jerusalem. How would they greet them and explain what they had seen?

How Far to Emmaus?

The two men who met Jesus on the Emmaus Road finally recognized him because of two things: First, they learned from the Scriptures with him; second, they worshiped with him—that is, Jesus prayed with them and broke the bread for them as he had at the Last Supper.

As a Christian, you want others also to have the best chance of knowing Christ and of having the fullness of life that Christ brings.

Think of walking the Emmaus Road as an image of coming to know Jesus Christ. Not only is it a journey, but it also suggests that people come to Christ through studying the Scriptures and participating in worship.

Think of your friends and other people whom you want to know Christ. How would you communicate to them your experience of the life that Christ gives? From the list below, what would you recommend for them? What about for yourself and your spiritual journey? What else would you recommend?

1. How often should they participate in opportunities for learning the Scriptures?

2. Where could they do so?

3. How often should they read the Scriptures, and for how long?

4. Where in the Bible should they start?

5. How often should they attend worship?

6. How often should they celebrate Holy Communion?

7. Should they have a time of worship (prayer and devotional reading) each day at home? If so, what should they do?

8. What is an acceptable reason for missing worship?

9. My ideas:

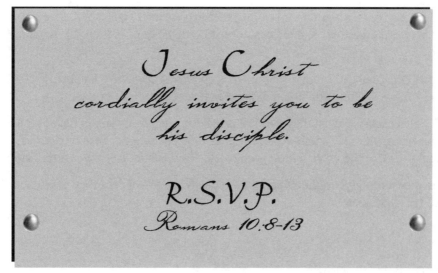

Jesus Christ cordially invites you to be his disciple.

R.S.V.P.
Romans 10:8-13

Session 26

The Great Promise

Say It Out Loud

Some things are easier to talk about than others. Certain topics we discuss only with family members, some things we confide in our best friend, and some things we can talk about with anyone. What are some things you find easy to talk about? What are some things you find difficult to talk about?

Here are some topics. Put an *E, C,* or *S* where appropriate in the **first blank** by each topic below.

E = This is an EASY topic to discuss with most anyone anytime.
C = I can discuss this only with CERTAIN people.
S = I really have to STRUGGLE to talk about this at all.

___ ___ 1. politics

___ ___ 2. my mother's pet name for me

___ ___ 3. my grades at school

___ ___ 4. what I got for my last birthday

___ ___ 5. Jesus

___ ___ 6. what I truly think of school

___ ___ 7. the most embarrassing thing that ever happened to me

___ ___ 8. how much I truly know about sex

___ ___ 9. who I'd like to date

___ ___ 10. my favorite junk food

___ ___ 11. the music I dislike the most

___ ___ 12. my prayer life

___ ___ 13. my shoe size

___ ___ 14. what my friends and I did last summer

___ ___ 15. what I want to do after high school

___ ___ 16. how I truly feel about my class picture

___ ___ 17. my religious uncertainties

___ ___ 18. my grade average

___ ___ 19. drug use among people I know

___ ___ 20. what I like on pizza

Go through the list again. This time put a *W* in the second blank by each topic that you WISH you could be more comfortable talking about.

Now go to the list one more time. Write the number of the topic you feel most comfortable with here _____, and the number of the topic you feel most uncomfortable with here _____.

Imagine what it would be like to have the same confidence for the second that you have for the first. In the space below, write down four ways you think your life would change if you could be that comfortable with the second. (You will not have to show this page to anyone if you do not wish to do so.)

1.

2.

3.

4.

Bible Study: Matthew 28:16-20

Matthew packs a lot into a few verses. His last five verses are meant to help us remember many things.

Verse 16. Matthew is careful to point out that only eleven disciples are present. How many disciples are usually mentioned?

Why do only eleven go to Galilee?

What do you think Matthew wants to remind his readers of by mentioning that only eleven disciples were present? *(Check as many as you agree with.)*

__ Judas had betrayed Jesus.

__ All of the disciples had betrayed Jesus.

__ The disciples weren't called because they were perfect but because Jesus loved them.

__ Even Matthew's readers need to beware of temptation.

The disciples had been sent to the mountains in Galilee to meet Jesus. Mountains play an important part in Matthew's Gospel. What other important events in Matthew take place on mountains? (If you can't remember, here are some clues: Matthew 4:8; 5:1; 17:1.)

What significant Old Testament event took place on a mountain, and whom did it involve? (Clue: See Exodus 19:20-20:17.)

Verse 17. When Jesus appeared on the mountain, what two things did the disciples do?

Which of those would you be most likely to do?

Verses 19-20. Jesus commands his disciples to do three things. What do you think they mean?

✐ "Make disciples of all nations"

✐ "Baptizing them"

✐ "Teaching them to obey everything that I have commanded you"

Verse 20. Jesus makes a promise to his disciples. What is it?

What might Matthew have wanted us to remember when he included Jesus' promise to the disciples? To find out, read Matthew 1:23 and see how the writer describes Jesus in the beginning of his Gospel. Then read Matthew 18:20 to see what important message Jesus gives his disciples.

✎ Matthew 1:23

✎ Matthew 18:20

Thought Questions

Do you remember how the disciples had behaved after the death of Jesus? They ran from him, denied him, and hid. They were surrounded by people who disliked them. If they had been left on their own, what do you think they would have done?

___ told everyone they met about Jesus
___ talked about Jesus only among themselves
___ hardly talked about Jesus at all

If they had not gone to Galilee and met Jesus there, how would they have felt eventually about their belief in Jesus?

___ mostly sad and disappointed
___ embarrassed
___ angry
___ proud but uncertain

We know from history and the Bible that the disciples were soon telling everyone, friends and strangers alike, about Jesus. What do you think influenced them most to do so?

___ Jesus was alive.
___ Jesus told them to do so.
___ Jesus promised to be with them.

Tell why you answered as you did.

What would help you be a better witness for Jesus—knowing that he was resurrected, knowing that he has told you to do so, or knowing that he will be with you no matter what happens? Why?